The Triumphs of Big Ben

The Triumphs of
Big Ben

by
JOHN DARWIN

ROBERT HALE · LONDON

© *John Darwin 1986*
First published in Great Britain 1986

Robert Hale Limited
Clerkenwell House
Clerkenwell Green
London EC1R 0HT

British Library Cataloguing in Publication Data
Darwin, John
The triumphs of Big Ben.
1. Big Ben (Clock)
I. Title
681.1'13   TS543.5.L6
<u>ISBN</u> 0-7090-2811-3 *501*

Set in Times Roman by
Rowland Phototypesetting Limited
Bury St Edmunds, Suffolk
and printed in Great Britain by
St Edmundsbury Press Limited, Bury St Edmunds, Suffolk
Bound by Hunter & Foulis Limited

Contents

*To the lovely lady who
once said she would blow up Big Ben
when she thought it imperilled the life of her husband*

List of Illustrations

List of figures

Foreword

by The Right Honourable Viscount Tonypandy PC

When I lived in Speaker's House, Westminster, Big Ben
towered just above me. I used to look out of the corridor
window in my private apartments and describe Big Ben as my
wristwatch. It has a majesty, a dignity and yet a special
friendliness of its own. There is nothing quite like Big Ben
anywhere else in the land, and for all I know anywhere else in
the world. Many a time in a foreign land the picture of Big
Ben has made me homesick.

Few people work in Parliament without developing a special affection for Big Ben. In the 1939–45 war the great boom
of its chime inspired freedom fighters in every occupied land
and thus matched the stirring challenge of Winston Churchill's speeches.

John Darwin, who for many years was Resident Engineer
and District Works Officer for the Palace of Westminster,
proves in this book that, like me, he loves every stone in the
building but has a very special feeling for Big Ben.

It was John Darwin's inspired leadership that spurred the
men who triumphed against odds in repairing Big Ben after its
major breakdown in 1976 and who got it working properly in
time for Her Majesty's Jubilee Visit to Westminster Hall in
1977.

With the ardent enthusiasm of someone researching his
own family history, John Darwin has probed into dark reces-
ses of history to provide a full, carefully documented story of
the life and times of Big Ben. I find this account both
fascinating and exciting. It is encouraging to read John Dar-

win's confident optimism that, 'With the present loving and devoted care, and the application of modern science to its preservation, there is every reason to expect that it will continue to operate, with distinction, for many centuries into the future and give pleasure and happiness to many generations of people.'

Our mighty Parliamentary heritage is enriched by John Darwin's labour of love in recording, for this and future generations, the dramatic story of the Great Clock.

I pray that those who serve the High Court of Parliament will ever remember that Big Ben is, and must always remain, a symbol of a Parliamentary democracy characterized by free speech and by the equality of all citizens before the law.

Tonypandy

Author's Preface

The clamour of the telephone at my bedside in the early hours found me so deeply asleep that it took me a few minutes before I could fully comprehend the great catastrophe that had occurred to the most famous clock in the world. Then I felt utterly drained of emotion, as if I had just heard of the death of a dear friend.

Although I had been assured the bomb squad had declared that there had been no explosion, notwithstanding the incredible damage, I rushed to my bathroom and gazed out to reassure myself. All the great Gothic windows of my residence above the Queen's Robing Room in the House of Lords faced the gardens and the river, and it was only from my bathroom that I could see the lovely south dial. What a relief to see that it appeared to be intact, although the hands were stopped at 3.45 a.m.

When I climbed some three hundred steps to the clock-room, I just could not believe that this scene of devastation had been caused by a mechanical failure. Great sections of the machinery, some weighing over a thousand pounds, had been torn from their bearings and hurled through the air, to smash against the stone walls; heavy portions of the huge gearwheels had driven clean through the timbered ceiling into the room above, the equipment and walls peppered with metal fragments and the windows broken. To all appearances the Great Clock would never work again.

In a lifetime of high adventure, as an engineer with the Royal Air Force in many parts of the world, I had always delighted in the variety of challenges which had come my way, especially when they approached the advanced boundaries of science, and in my retirement post as Resident Engineer of the Palace of Westminster I welcomed the unexpected opportunity of tackling the engineering task of restoring this enormous antique clock to London and the sound of the chimes to the multitudes of listeners throughout the world. Yet the task of repair appeared so formidable that, on that morning, it was almost beyond comprehension that it might be possible to reclaim even part of the mechanism from the wreckage. The prospect of restarting any section seemed unutterably remote.

But Big Ben is not only antique: it is utterly unique. Since the earliest days of its creation it was surrounded by great difficulties and bitter controversies (some of which were to sow the seeds of this disaster). From before the start it was bedevilled by bureaucracy, attacked by vested interest and delayed by political changes, as well as having its development hampered by the inadequacies of the age in materials and techniques. Notwithstanding all this, Big Ben triumphed, to become the largest and most accurate public clock of the nineteenth century.

So it was essential to do the impossible. By superhuman efforts by all concerned, the least damaged parts of the mechanism were patched up and, perched precariously on two three-ton jacks, it was possible to restart the hands. Although silent, Big Ben was again able to tell the time, with its customary accuracy, by four o'clock in the afternoon of the day of the disaster. Neither I nor anyone else could then foresee the full extent of the difficulties that lay ahead.

I was not a trained horologist, but the restoration and preservation of the clock were basically scientific and engineering matters calling for the blending of many specialist skills with firm management.

In this so many played a part: Sir Robert Cooke and his Commons Committee, with their steadfast encouragement; the DOE staff in the Palace, the National Physical Laboratory staff, the Testing Staff of the Atomic Energy Authority and, most especially, Thwaites & Reed – all achieving the impossible. So Big Ben triumphed once more.

This book traces the history of how, through many disasters, it has 'triumphed over Death and Chance, and thee O Time' to become the most famous clock in the world.

John Darwin

Introduction

The deep, mellow notes of Big Ben, echoing through West-minster, have the power to stir the heart, to inspire love and affection and a deep sense of peace and stability, not only in the peoples of these islands but also, through the British Broadcasting Corporation, throughout the world. Millions of people in hundreds of nations know and love the sounds of the great bells. Many of them have no knowledge of our English tongue but they recognize the voice of Big Ben, and the deep tones seem to have a power to move everyone to look beyond their own little circle to a wider sphere. It is not just the symbol of Britain; for many it covers the greater aspirations of

> A land of settled government,
> A land of just and old renown,
> Where Freedom slowly broadens down,
> From precedent to precedent.
>
> *Tennyson*

Perhaps these ideas originated, for many, back in the wartime years when it was the tongue of freedom, of hope, of the idea of a free and unfettered democracy, and when the 'Big Ben Minute' spoke of unity and love.

But for many more young people, Who have not these memories, it is still the same deep, familiar sound which they have heard all their lives and have learnt to love, and which they feel belongs to them.

The great complexity of the charm of both the sound and visual image of Big Ben is such that it appeals to each individual in a different way. To some it is the image of

Parliament, to others it is associated with the nightly news on television; to the tourist it is the heart of London, to the politician or the cartoonist of the world it is the emblem of Britain, as the Statue of Liberty is of the USA; to children it may remind them of their first toys. But to so many it is a special combination of all these things, with more added.

Perhaps this is why, when the Great Clock was mute following the catastrophe of 1976, so many letters poured in from all over the world. Some were from adults wishing to catch the next plane from Texas or the Middle East to come and help to restore Big Ben. But many more were from children who missed the old familiar notes and wrote to Big Ben as a dear friend who was ill.

Yet Big Ben was conceived, designed and constructed in strife and some of the bitterest controversy of the times. It has been said that the greatest and best human characters were nurtured and moulded by hard times and harsh realities as well as by deep love and affection. Perhaps this is also true of Big Ben. Without the fierce fires of all the angry quarrels and disputes, the strong antagonisms and stronger reprisals, there might not have grown the robustness of character and the strength which enabled Big Ben to win the love and devotion necessary to achieve the many triumphs of its long career. Indeed, it was these very qualities which enabled Big Ben, in the world of today, to triumph over the disaster which had its roots deep in the decisions forced upon its creators by the constraints and hindrances engendered by these old discords. Destiny moulds character, and in turn character reaps destiny.

THE NAME OF BIG BEN

Every character requires a name, and Big Ben was to acquire one even before the clock struck the first hour. Perhaps this arose from tradition as well as from affection. From time immemorial all large bells had acquired special nicknames and indeed, to some degree, were given personalities, generated no doubt by the high clamour of their tones dominating their surroundings.

The name Big Ben was first given to the great bell only, but over the long years it has spread to encompass not only the whole of the clock and its mechanism but also the clocktower and even the adjoining locality. Thus if a Member tells another that he will meet him 'under Big Ben', he means at the foot of the clocktower. The use has even spread across the road, and each year Westminster Abbey holds a special series of services entitled 'Under Big Ben' although held, of course, in the precincts. This broadening of the appellation has been given respectability and ratification by being used by many Speakers of the House of Commons.

There were stories that, at the time of the building, it was intended that the clocktower should be called the Albert Tower, to complement the greater Victoria Tower on the south side of the Palace. Possibly there were some disagreements about this proposal, as Prince Albert was never without his opponents in the Commons, but before the clocktower was completed, the deep notes of Big Ben had ensured that no other name could dominate the Palace of Westminster.

There are many and varied stories of the origin of the name. The earliest goes back to shortly after the delivery of the first great bell to New Palace Yard in 1856, when it was seen to bear the following inscription: 'Cast on the 20th, year of the reign of Her Majesty Queen Victoria, and in the Year of Our Lord 1856; from the design of Edmund Beckett Denison Q.C. Sir Benjamin Hall MP Chief Commissioner of Works.' It is claimed by some that men on site, seeing the name Benjamin on the bell and impressed with its great size, first called it 'Big Ben'.

There is also the story that during a minor discussion in the Chamber of the House of Commons one afternoon there were some suggestions for the naming of the bell. It was related that, when Sir Benjamin Hall was replying on behalf of the government, an unnamed Member interposed to say, 'Why not call it Big Ben?' This caused much laughter and acclamation, as Sir Benjamin was six feet four inches tall and of a vast girth. Unfortunately there is no record in Hansard of this remark or of any reply from Sir Benjamin.

At this time there was a famous pugilist, Benjamin Caunt (who had adopted the name 'Big Ben' from an even more famous fighter of the 1780s) who fought a drawn contest of sixty rounds against Benigo in 1858. Maybe the nicknaming of the great bell being tested in New Palace Yard was influenced by a name that was on the lips of many at that time.

Whichever was the true origin of the name, there is ample evidence that it was seized by all the newspapers of the day and that they spread the use of the name throughout the country.

1　A Visit to Big Ben

'All rising to great place is by a winding stair.'
Francis Bacon

The clocktower is not open to the general public at the time of writing. It is, of course, a privileged part of a most important royal palace, and for that reason alone entrance has to be restricted. Also, unfortunately, in this day and age the element of security cannot be overlooked. This was brought home vividly a few years ago, when the clocktower seemed to tremble at the violent explosion which murdered Airey Neave MP as his car was ascending the ramp from the car-park, only a few yards from the base of the clocktower.

Another important factor is that the provision of an adequate lift, together with the necessary toilet facilities, would certainly cost over a quarter of a million pounds, and even then the space available for the lift would mean that parties would need to be restricted to very small numbers. It is possible for Members of either of the Houses of Parliament to arrange for small parties to visit the clock and bells, but of course such visits need to be limited, and each party must be guided. As there are some 350 steps to climb, such visits are not suitable for the elderly or invalids; and children under eleven years of age are not admitted.

Notwithstanding these difficulties, requests for visits are very numerous, and Bill Anderson, who guided parties until his recent retirement, achieved distinction in the *Guinness Book of Records* for having ascended the clocktower more than two thousand times, climbing over two million steps.

It is usual for parties to leave the foot of the clocktower at not later than half past the hour. This is to enable them to be in the clockroom at the time the clock chimes the quarter to the hour and to be up in the belfry in time to watch, as well as hear, the full chimes and the striking of the hour, which is always most impressive. If possible, it is advantageous to arrive early and spend a few minutes walking along Bridge Street towards the foot of the tower, to enjoy by actual inspection the beauty of the newly cleaned stonework, so often seen from a distance or on television. It is remarkable how many artists have tried to portray the clocktower, and how very few have managed to get the proportions exactly right, or to recapture the elegant grace of this masterpiece of the Barry/Pugin genius. As you pass the foot of the tower, you will see a stone plaque which commemorates the centenary of Big Ben, but as you are going up the clock, there is no need to strain to read the inscription as there is a replica of it in wood on display in the clockroom.

After entering through the Carriage Gates, you will pass around New Palace Yard, so called as it was the yard of the new palace built by William II (William Rufus) in 1088, whose Westminster Hall you will pass on your right. At the foot of the clocktower, you will be admitted by the guide. The climb up the long, winding staircase is hard work, and it is advisable to take it very slowly, with frequent pauses for short rests. Contrary to expectations, the first hundred steps are usually the most trying part, because in this area all the windows are bricked up and there are no doors. Later, when you come to the windows, there is every excuse to stop and admire the views, whilst you are recovering your breath.

The windows in the first section are bricked up because some of them shut off prison cells. It is not always remembered that the two Houses carry all the duties and privileges of the High Court of Parliament, and in the past it was a not infrequent event for offenders against the rights and privileges of Parliament to be brought before the Bar of the House. Unless they purged their contempt by an abject apology, required for many centuries to be delivered kneeling, they were marched off by the Serjeant at Arms (who always wears a sword when on duty in the Chamber) and held in imprisonment in the cells which were accessible only through his residence in the House of Commons. In general Members of Parliament were held in these cells only overnight, but history relates that a Lord Mayor of London was once detained in the parliamentary cells for a week – but this was before Big Ben. The sounds of Big Ben, booming so close above, must have disturbed the troubled sleep of those imprisoned who were wondering what the future was to bring. If the offence was so grave that further imprisonment was decreed, the offender was usually conveyed to the Tower of London, where at least his sleep would be less disturbed! Imprisonment was usually terminated by a resolution of the House but if not terminated earlier would automatically end with the session of the House.

The last Member to be detained in the cells of Big Ben was Charles Bradlaugh, who refused to take the Oath of Allegiance in 1880, on the grounds that the oath was to God, and he was an atheist. He was therefore arraigned at the Bar of the House and committed to the cells for Contempt of Parliament. Following his imprisonment his seat was declared vacant and he had to stand in a bye-election, at which he was re-elected, but this time the House accepted his Affirmation of Allegiance and he was allowed to take his seat. Since then such declarations have readily been accepted, and no occasion has occurred which has warranted the detention of a Member or other important person. It will, of course, be recognized that these cells are only for Members, and their equivalents: more normal, if less historic, cells are available below Royal Court, for the detention of offenders who are not Members, and these are still used fairly frequently, although serious cases are taken to nearby Cannon Row police station.

Leaving behind the gloomy thoughts occasioned by the blank windows of the prison cell area, the long climb is relieved by a number of doors to small rooms. These doors are always locked, but the rooms inside are cold and bare and generally unsuitable for habitation. Apart from the storage of the stone ballast put in to ensure the stability of the clock-tower, other rooms contain stone carving details which have come loose, and two of them hold pieces of the clock mechanism which were broken in the catastrophe of 1976. The many windows show views of all the roofs of the Palace spread below, and the beauty of the Central Tower and beyond it the massive proportions and gay pinnacles of the Victoria Tower.

It is also refreshing to pause to glance down at the busy traffic in Bridge Street.

THE DIALS

After climbing some 290 steps, there is a narrow doorway which leads to the spaces behind the dials. It is only when one is able to walk around behind the four dials that it is possible to comprehend fully the immense size and the filigree beauty of the mosaic lattice of cast iron and opaline glass. These dials were designed by that master of the neo-Gothic, Augustus Welby Pugin, who alas did not live to see the completion of the clock. (Plate I)

It was Pugin who persuaded the architect Barry that his original idea of having clock faces thirty feet in diameter was too large for the height of the clock and gained his agreement to reduce the size to twenty-three feet. Even this was far larger than the figure which would have resulted from the application of the old clockmaker's rule-of-thumb guide: that the dial should be one foot in diameter for every twelve feet in height of the clock centre above ground level, which would have resulted in dials just over fifteen feet in diameter. However in this, as in so many other issues, Pugin's taste was impeccable, and the dials, although vastly larger than those of any other clockface then in existence, are just right for the size and shape of the clocktower.

The Gothic style made each face a beautiful cast-iron tracery, containing 312 irregular panes of opalescent glass, incorporating the minute marks, each one foot square, and the numerals, each two foot high. The unusual calligraphy of Pugin's Gothic numerals still raises annual enquiries from Members and others on their derivation. It is interesting to note that the cost of the dials was more than that of the clock mechanism and the bells combined.

The external faces of the dials are normally cleaned every three years. Although there are removable panes in the tracery, to allow access to the central boss of the hands for lubrication, these are not large enough to permit cleaning the dials, so windowcleaners are lowered from the belfry floor above in cradles. It is a task which has to be done with some care to prevent the men and cradles touching the hands and so slowing or stopping the clock. A minor piece of undesirable publicity occurred in the cleaning of the faces before Her Majesty the Queen's Silver Jubilee, when an unscrupulous lady journalist bribed the windowcleaners to open the removable panes and put their heads out, to enable her to photograph the heads appearing through the dial of Big Ben.

It is possible to walk round all four faces, inside the glass, and it is rather like walking past the great windows of a cathedral. At night time it is even more impressive (although visitors are never admitted at night), as one is enveloped in the tremendous flood of light which makes the faces visible, on a clear night, from as far away as Hampstead Heath. Initially the lighting was by gas flares, which were simply jets which burned the gas with no premixing of air so that it had a yellow smoky flame; afterwards fish-tail burners were installed, but it was forty years before the newly invented gas mantles could be used. There was the suggestion at that time (1900) that electric lighting could be used but it was argued that it was necessary to retain gas lighting so that the heat from the burners could prevent snow and ice forming on the hands. Even with the new mantles the illumination was inadequate, and in the year 1906 a simple scheme for electrification was installed, using ten ordinary hundred-watt bulbs behind each face. This avoided having to send a man up the clocktower every night to light the gas, whilst the low efficiency of this form of lighting gave off enough heat to prevent the accumulation of ice except during the very coldest winter weather.

In 1957 an installation of cold cathode lights was provided which gave a vastly greater illumination with less energy consumption. This system, which is still giving excellent service today, had the further advantage that, as the normal tube life is over ten thousand hours, it also represented a saving of maintenance labour. The higher efficiency, however, meant that there was less waste heat to prevent ice forming on the hands, so small electric heaters had to be installed behind the north and east dials.

THE CLOCKROOM

On leaving the great dials, there are only a few further steps up to the clockroom, which is housed within the great square of the dials. At first sight it appears a surprisingly large room, and one is inclined to wonder at the disputes on the size in the early construction period, for it is thirty-six feet long by about sixteen feet in height and width. This size, although greater than that originally offered by Barry, was not the greatest difficulty; this arose from the desirability of getting the mechanism as close as possible to the centre of the square of the faces, which was obstructed by the structural walls of the central core. It was this that prevented the fly fans being mounted in the conventional manner.

The room is completely dominated by the mechanism of the clock, which is vastly greater than anything that could be expected. The large size of the mechanism, which is fifteen feet five inches long by four feet eleven inches wide, was dictated by the requirements of the Astronomer Royal's specification, which called for the clock to be made of cast iron (instead of the usual brass) and required it to be built so that any of the large gearwheels could be removed without disturbing the rest.

The loud 'tick' of the mechanism every two seconds, caused by the pendulum activating the escapement (the device which allows the energy of the weights to escape to turn the hands) dominates the room and imposes a degree of solemnity on all those entering, almost as effectively as does the atmosphere of some great cathedral or mausoleum, in that it tends to subdue conversations. It is almost as if it was the tick of doom, measuring with its sound the short lifespan of man.

There are railings around the mechanism to prevent spectators getting too close and to safeguard them from any danger of being caught up in the huge gearwheels. Standing near these railings it will be seen that the very long bedplate of the clock bridges the space between two masonry pedestals; on this bedplate is mounted the basic mechanism of the movement with gearing going up to the shafts which drive the hands; and high above the two great flyfans and the cables going up to the belfry to operate the bells. Somewhat harder to see are the cables going down below the bedplate to the weights below. The front of the bedplate bears the following inscription in cast-iron letters: 'THIS CLOCK WAS MADE IN THE YEAR OF OUR LORD 1854 BY FREDERICK DENT OF THE STRAND AND THE ROYAL EX-CHANGE, CLOCKMAKER TO THE QUEEN, FROM

THE DESIGNS OF EDMUND BECKETT DENISON Q.C.' Below the bedplate is a small cast-iron plate inscribed simply: 'FIXED HERE 1859'. This is to mark the fact that it was not possible to install the mechanism of the clock for five years after its manufacture as it was waiting for progress on the clocktower, which had been started in 1843.

Facing the clock mechanism (see Plate II) from behind the guardrails, it will be seen that there are three interlinked trains of gears and drums, a large one at each end and a smaller one in the middle. This smaller train in the centre is known as the 'going train' because it is the heart of the clock which makes it 'go'. Despite its relatively small size, it is the engine which provides all the energy to drive the hands and sustain the pendulum. In addition it controls the operation of the two other trains which drive the bells. It is powered by a five-hundredweight cast-iron weight, suspended on a pulley in the weight shaft, with one end of the cable anchored at the top and the other coiled round the small drum, seen in the centre, which turns the train of gears under the control of the pendulum through the escapement.

Behind this central part of the mechanism, it is possible, by going round to the side, to see a small part of the pendulum. The greater part of its thirteen-foot six-inch length is enclosed in the pendulum pit, which is a cast-iron box let into the floor of the clockroom to shield the pendulum from draughts. It is possible to see the suspension (known as the pendulum cock) and the suspension spring, which is a small flexible piece of spring steel which allows the pendulum to swing. The pendulum cock is a massive casting which is mounted on a very solid masonry wall and has no contact with the rest of the mechanism, except through the 'escapement'. The swinging of the pendulum, as it touches the very light arms of the escapement, allows the energy from the weights to pass to the hands and at the same time receives a slight pressure of less than one ounce, from the 'going train' to sustain the pendulum in motion. The accuracy of the clock is determined by the pendulum and the escapement, so more will be said about this in a later chapter. Before leaving the pendulum, one should note the boss or coupling joining the top and lower part of the pendulum. It is on here that pennies are placed to give a very fine control in making the clock gain or lose time.

The energy of the going train, as released by the pendulum, through the escapement, is fed to the hands through bevel gearing and shafting which takes it up to the gantry some four feet above the bedplate of the clock, where, through another train of gears, it feeds the four arbors (shafts) which go out in the direction of the central bosses of the hands. These arbors move so slowly that they appear stationary, and on more than one occasion, despite specific warnings, painters have rested their ladders against one of them and so stopped the clock.

On the left-hand side of the mechanism is the 'striking train', so called because it provides the energy for the striking of the great hour bell (the one originally called Big Ben) by the raising and releasing of its four-hundredweight hammer. To provide this energy the train needs to be vastly larger than the going train, although that was the heart of the clock, and it needs a much larger weight to store the energy to lift the hammer 156 times a day. In fact, there is a one-ton weight, suspended in the weight shaft in the same way as the weight of the going train, with a very stout steel cable which turns on the massive striking drum. When released by the trigger from the going train, the drum is allowed to turn, and the very heavy cams at the rear of the drum raise and suddenly release a stout cast-iron lever, visible at the extreme left side of the bedplate, which is attached to the cable which lifts and releases the heavy hammer on the great bell. The number of strokes is controlled by a rotating locking plate, which is slotted to enable the locking arm to rotate only the correct number of times. The speed of striking is governed by one of the two 'flyfans' which occupy so much of the space above the gantry.

The flyfan for the striking mechanism consists of two large sheets of metal, each about ten square feet in area, mounted on either side of a vertical metal arbor (shaft) some ten feet above the clock bedplate. This flyfan, which is rotated by the drum through a pair of bevel gears, is of great importance as it acts as an air brake, to keep the speed of rotation of the striking drum uniform and to allow for equal intervals between the strokes. In fact, it acts as a governor on the striking train. The great size of the flyfan, which is commensurate with the size of the bell hammer, should be noted, and so should its unusual position so far above the clock. In virtually all large chiming clocks the flyfans for the bells are mounted horizontally and very close to the mechanism. When Denison first designed the clock, he incorporated the flyfans, mounted horizontally, on the mechanism. When he was first permitted to visit the clocktower, he discovered that the existing structural walls made the mounting of the flyfans in the conventional manner impossible. This necessitated a change in design which was to have its consequences in the great catastrophe of 1976.

On the right-hand side of the mechanism is the 'chiming' train, so called because it provides energy for the chiming of the four quarter bells. It is very similar to the striking train in size and layout, except that the cam arrangements are larger and more complex as they need to operate five bell ropes, and the weight in the shaft is 1¼ tons. Questions are sometimes asked as to why the chiming train should need a larger weight as it has to lift very much smaller hammers. It will be remembered, however, that the chiming train has to lift forty small hammers an hour – that is, 960 in a complete day – whilst the striking train has only to lift 156 heavy hammers in the same period. It is thus necessary for the weight to be heavy enough to store sufficient energy to operate these bells for at least half a week. It will be observed by some that there are five operating cables, whilst there are only four bells, but the reason for this will be seen when visiting the belfry.

The chiming train must start operating for the four-chime series before the clock strikes the hour, at least twenty seconds before the exact time, to enable the long chime to complete and the sound to die away before the first stroke of the hour bell gives the precise time. The trigger mechanism of the going train must therefore be set accordingly to make this allowance at the full hour only. The other quarter hour chimes must be set to be as exactly on the quarter as possible, although the need for exact accuracy is less than at the hour. Each of the quarter hour chimes is different as shown in the musical score (Fig. 1), so that it is possible to decide which quarter it is without hearing the complete chime. The levers which operate the five cables from the cams are much smaller but more complex than the single lever on the striking train. The speed of release and the regulation of the intervals between the strokes of the chimes are governed by an even

𝔓alace of 𝔚estminster
𝔠himes

of the

𝔊reat 𝔠lock

1   Chimes

larger flyfan than is required for striking, although the selection of the chimes is determined by a similar but more complex notched locking plate.

It will be recalled that the visit was timed to give visitors sufficient time to climb the winding stair, see behind the dials and settle into the clockroom before the mechanism chimes the three-quarters of an hour. It is sometimes advisable to remind them that it is coming, because in the clockroom the chiming of the quarter bells can be quite alarming, not from the sound of the bells but from the noise of the mechanism; having accepted the loud and solemn tick of the clock, the other sounds can appear dangerous, unless warned in advance. The first shock comes from a very loud click from the locking lever, a minute in advance. This is known as 'the warning', as it is intended to warn anyone working on or near the mechanism to get clear before the chiming begins. This sudden noise startles visitors, who are inclined to wonder if the great mechanism has gone wrong.

After the 'warning' has sounded, there seems a long minute of comparative hush – broken only by the solemn ticking of the clock – until the great wheels begin to turn. It is the flyfan above, which seems to make most noise to begin with, as it whirs around, punctuated by the thuds of the hammers operated by the cams, which jerk and release the five bell ropes of the chiming train. The chiming bells can be heard from above, but in the clockroom their music is somewhat muffled by the thick walls so that the noise from the mechanism predominates. For the three-quarters of an hour chime, each of the four bells is struck three times, and at the end of these chimes every other noise is drowned out by the tremendous sound from the ratchet at the top of the flyfan, which makes a din like a great fairground rattle and causes some visitors to feel nervous.

Before leaving the clockroom, many visitors see the large winding handles on the striking and chiming trains and ask how the clock is wound. This is a rather complex process, with special maintaining gear, and for those of a scientific turn of mind the full procedure is outlined in Appendix III. For those less interested in detail, it is perhaps sufficient to say that it is possible to wind up either the striking or the chiming gear by using those handles, but it is very hard work and takes two men some three hours to wind each side. This was the way in which the clock was wound for more than the first fifty years, with much toil three times a week. The clock is still wound three times a week but since 1912 the heavy work has been done by a small electric motor-driven gear which can be connected to wind up any of the three weights which motivate the three sections of the mechanism. Even this method takes some thirty to forty minutes for each of the larger trains, and it is customary to wind up the small going train by hand, which takes only some fifteen minutes, whilst the other trains are being machine wound. The operator spends the remainder of the time oiling and doing minor maintenance to the mechanism, checking the accuracy of the clock and keeping records, which are stored in the cupboard and may be seen by serious horological students.

In leaving the clockroom there is time to glance quickly at two boards which are mounted on the wall. One was used as a prototype for the stone which was let into the base of the clocktower, for the centenary celebrations in 1959, and reads:

1859 – 1959
This stone commemorates the Centenary of
Big Ben and the Great Clock of Westminster.

The other oaken board give the words, in a suitable Gothic script, that are traditionally linked by Members with the music of the chimes:

All through this Hour,
Lord be my Guide,
That by Thy Power,
No foot should slide.

'The music of the chimes is taken from Handel's Messiah.'

THE BELFRY

Following the chiming of the three-quarters of the hour, there is ample time to climb the forty steps up to the belfry before the hour strikes. On the way up there is a hatch door into the lever room which contains the many cranks which position the cables from the mechanism beneath the hammer mechanisms of the appropriate bells. This room is not open to visitors as there is little to see, and the height from floor to ceiling is only about four feet, so movement is difficult.

Emerging through the door into the belfry, the first impression is that of being buffeted by the winds, as even on a calm day the currents of air which so often follow the line of the river give the impression that the belfry is wide open to all the winds of heaven. Actually the belfry is enclosed with a screening of link fencing, within the Gothic open tracery, which is designed to prevent pigeons nesting – not, as has been said, 'to prevent Big Ben getting bats in the belfry'. This is effective in its objective but gives little protection from the weather. Having become accustomed to the wind, the next impression is of the enormous size and mass of the bells.

There is a small gantry along the side of the great bell, and from there it is remarkable how large even the quarter bells look, especially the two which are hanging just above one's head. Indeed, one of them weighs four tons and would seem enormous were it not dwarfed by the size of the Big Ben bell.

After a few minutes one can tear one's eyes away from the great bells and glance at the panorama of London life which is spread below. From this height the river craft and the cars crossing the river bridges look like toys; on the other side Westminster Abbey enables one to visualize the extent of what used to be the monastic outbuildings and domestic quarters, which have now been partly transformed into West-minster School and Church House, with all the clergy accom-modation around Dean's Yard. As the eye roves over St James's Park towards Buckingham Palace and all the Minis-tries of Whitehall, all is suddenly wiped from one's mind by the unbelievable clamour of the quarter bells clanging out the chimes so close above one's head. Here in the belfry there is no warning click, as in the clockroom; suddenly all around is dominated by the strident clash of the loud music of these bells. It has made some visitors almost jump out of their skins, and young children have been known to curl up in a ball and be very upset. (That is one of the reasons why access to the clocktower has been restricted to older children.) The deep, mellow booms of the great bell which follow the chimes are very much louder, but by then the instantaneous surprise and shock of the first impact of the waves of sound have died away and the ear is more adapted to very high sound-levels.

To ensure precision of the time given by the bells, it is not usual for clock bells to be swung in the manner adopted by many church bells with the object of calling the faithful to prayer. The swinging of the whole bell, with an internal clapper to make the music, certainly gives a glorious euphony which can gladden the heart. The Big Ben bell came fitted with a clapper, which hung from the centre of the interior until 1934, but of course the bell was far too big to be swung, even if there had been any wish to do so, as a swinging weight of this magnitude, however well balanced, would soon have caused the clocktower to disintegrate. All the bells are struck with hammers, but it is most essential that the hour bell be struck at precisely the right second.

The F Natural bell has two hammers, whilst all the others have only one. This is because this bell needs to be struck twice during the second and fourth quarter chimes, and the timing would not permit one hammer to operate twice at the interval required; this is the reason for the fifth bell cable which was seen in the clockroom.

The hammers of the quarter bells come to rest about a quarter of an inch away from the skirt of the bell; this is the usual custom to allow the bell to resonate freely without being dampened by the hammer touching it. On the Big Ben bell, however, the heavy hammer moves back a full nine inches. This is to assist in the accuracy of the first stroke, which must be precisely on the hour.

Some years ago this wide spacing of the hammer on the Big Ben bell was a temptation to a party of schoolboys, who were allowed to visit the clock and bells accompanied by their schoolmaster and the guide. After their visit was over and the next hour came around, the chimes sounded as usual, but afterwards the great bell produced only a dull thud instead of its customary clear note. The engineers climbed the clock-tower with some apprehension, fearing that someone might have been caught in the bell mechanism. At the end of their 340-stair climb, however, they discovered the reason for Big Ben's dull thud. These naughty schoolboys, with dire intent, had chewed a prodigious amount of chewing gum. Whilst some of their number distracted the attention of their school-master and the guide by asking questions, one of them had slipped away, taking with him all the chewing gum, which they had pooled, and stuck the great mass firmly onto the centre of the hammer of the Big Ben bell! So these wretched boys had succeeded in their prank of silencing Big Ben – let us hope that their schoolmaster dealt with the matter in an appropriate manner! With some difficulty all the chewing gum was scraped away, and Big Ben was able to strike the next hour with its normally clear musical note. After this, barriers were provided to prevent any repetition of this incident.

An examination of the surface of the great bell will show that there is a slot cut in the edge of the skirt, and the fine line of a crack running down towards it. This was the slot which was cut to prevent the crack spreading further; that it was successful is shown by the fact that the crack did not develop, and indeed it has not been necessary to take any further measurements for more than a century. Near to it is a square hole in the surface of the bell, where the metal was chipped out to enable Dr Percy to make his chemical analysis of the composition of the bell-metal, which he found to be over-rich in tin, which was the cause of the crack. Nowadays we are rather surprised at the size of the sample taken, which seems enormous compared with the tiny slivers of metal which are all that are now needed. But then 130 years ago analytical chemistry was just beginning.

In a corner of the belfry is a cast-iron spiral staircase leading aloft, which is always closed to visitors. If it were possible to ascend this staircase, it would lead to the platform from which the bells are suspended in their massive 'collars' which fit round the necks of the bells and allow them that small degree of freedom so that they can resonate clearly. The massive cast-iron beams with their multitude of large rivets, which make the framework for the support of the bells and also arch their way up into the spire, invite attention and remind us that the constructions was done in an age of iron, when steel was expensive and available only in small quantities. The whole structural skeleton of the new palace was made of cast iron and, at a time when there were no scientific methods for detecting blow-holes, each girder had to be tested individually on site by simple means, before they could be riveted together to form these great structures, which are still in such a good state of preservation. On this floor too are the microphones from which the sound of the bells is broadcast to the world.

THE AYRTON LIGHT

If it were possible to proceed further up the spiral staircase, one would come to the signal lantern, above the clock, which tells Members of Parliament and the people of London that either one or both of the Houses of Parliament are sitting. It is called the Ayrton Light after A. S. Ayrton MP, First Commissioner of Works 1869–73, who advocated this feature. It was not installed until 1885, and then it was visible only in west London. This limited visibility caused discontent among Members living in other districts, and it was replaced in

1892–3 by the present lantern, which is nine feet in diameter and twelve feet high with all-round visibility.

The lantern, 254 feet above ground level, was originally illuminated by gas with sixty-eight simple gas-burners so placed that their gas jets merged into a solid mass of flame in the centre of the lantern. It was vastly uneconomical, consuming no less than 240 cubic feet of gas an hour. The flame had to be ignited by a man climbing the long flights of stairs up to the Ayrton Light, every day at sunset, although it was arranged that it could be extinguished (when the Speaker left his Chair in the Commons, to the cry of 'Who Goes Home?', or when the Lord Chancellor left the Woolsack of the Lords, and processed round in solemn state to his residence) by operating a valve in the Engineer's Control Room. This system of using a gas flame was replaced, with great economy, by a cluster of 150-watt lamps in 1903, which meant that all switching could be done from the control room and there was no need for anyone to make the long climb.

The procedure, for many years, was that, when the flag on the Victoria Tower, which is flown every day when either of the Houses of Parliament is to sit, was lowered at sunset, the Ayrton Light was lit. It remained on until both the Houses had risen or, in the event of an all-night sitting, until the flag was raised at 8 a.m. the following morning. In 1978 this procedure was varied as a result of Members emerging from their rooms in Westminster after 8 a.m. being confused and thinking that the House had risen and the flag was up as usual for the next day's proceedings, whilst actually the all-night sitting was still in session and their presence might be required. The revised procedure is that now, when there is an all-night sitting, the Ayrton Light is kept on until the House rises, even if the flag has been raised.

The Ayrton Light is not the highest point which can be reached in the clocktower. There are vertical iron ladders going up from there to the very apex of the spire, but these are somewhat hazardous and are used only for very occasional maintenance inspections. Londoners and people from many nations like to see the Ayrton Light, high above Big Ben, and sometimes appreciate that the Commons are sitting long hours to debate the nation's business. Few of them are aware, however, that the proceedings of the House of Commons take such a vastly greater time than those of any similar assembly anywhere else in the world, or indeed that it might be that the Lords are burning the midnight oil after the Commons had risen.

Big Ben can look most beautiful at night. The clocktower was among the first buildings in London to be floodlit for the International Illumination Congress of 1–27 September 1931. Subsequently it was illuminated for the Silver Jubilee of King George V in 1935, the Coronation of King George VI in 1937, and the Victory Celebrations in 1945–6. Beginning with the Festival of Britain in 1951, Big Ben has been floodlit every summer, except 1956–7 when it was scaffolded for repairs. Since 1964 the floodlighting has been kept on throughout the year, but with shut-off at 11 p.m. in winter instead of midnight. Up to 1970 the floodlighting was by 1,000-watt projectors, but on 31 December 1970 a new system was installed using high-pressure sodium lighting which gives a warm golden glow to the stone of the tower. This is embellished with mercury discharge lamps giving a bluish/green contrasting colour to the belfry. In addition to producing very much more light and making Big Ben even more of a landmark in London, and on television screens throughout the world, this was a spectacular piece of energy conservation, as it reduced the electrical loading from 135 kilowatts to fifteen. This scheme was awarded a silver trophy in 1972 as the most beautiful floodlighting in England. Since then the two other towers and the terrace of the Palace have also been floodlit. During part of 1976 a laser beam from the Covent Garden area, some two miles away, was directed on the finial on the top of the clocktower, which made the golden 'ball and shower of stars' which terminate the clocktower light up and glow a brilliant green like a radiant display of priceless emeralds.

On the long descent from the belfry there is ample time to pause to glance through the long needle windows at the beauty of the Victoria Tower, once the tallest and still the most elegant square tower in the world. The loveliness of the Central (St Stephen's) Tower is striking, and it is strange to think that it was put in as a ventilating duct. Nor can one overlook the hundreds of carved pinnacles on the Palace roofs, many of which serve also as ventilators.

2 The Old Clock Tower, Palace Yard in about 1700

2 Big Ben's Ancestor – 'Great Tom'

Brutus: Peace! Count the clock.
Cassius: The clock has stricken three.
Shakespeare, *Julius Caesar*

No story of Big Ben would be complete without a mention of the first great clock to stand in New Palace Yard and which might be called the ancestor of the present clock and bells. It is believed by many that this was the very first public clock ever erected in Britain, but there are others who consider that, although it is likely to have been the first on a purely secular edifice, there were probably clocks, striking the hours but without dials or hands, on early ecclesiastic buildings.

The origins of this very early clock are given in a well-authenticated story that in the year 1288 a Lord Chief Justice of the King's Bench, Sir Ralph de Hengham, had a Court Roll entry erased, to reduce the fine on a poor person, a friend of his, from 13s. 4d. to 6s. 8d, following a court sitting in Westminster Hall. Inevitably this alteration was brought to the notice of King Edward I, who decreed that a very heavy fine of 800 marks (at that time a Lord Chief Justice received only 70 marks per annum) be imposed on Sir Ralph and the proceeds devoted to the building of a clocktower in New Palace Yard. The clock was required to have one dial (facing the Palace) and a bell, so that the sounding of the hours should remind the Justices sitting in Westminster Hall of the gravity of Sir Ralph's offence and to bring home to them the necessity of probity in all their duties.

The records of the building of the clocktower and mechanism were probably destroyed in the great fire of 1299, and we have no information on the mechanism. It is believed that there was only a single hand and that round the dial was an inscription from Virgil: 'Discite Justitiam Moniti' – which can roughly be translated as 'Learn the Justice of My Advice'. Nearly a century later there are accounts for the payments to a builder, under the supervision of Henry Yevele (who also restored Westminster Hall), for the rebuilding of the stone tower, and the payment for a great bell inscribed 'Edward of Westminster'.

At that time there were very few clocks and no watches, so this clock served an important public need, both in the King's Court and for the population generally. Whether it entirely met its original purpose of ensuring the impartial administration of justice is perhaps open to question, although the old example did have some power in the time of Queen Elizabeth I, when it was proposed by one judge to another that an alteration of the records should be made. His fellow judge is reported to have said, 'Brother, I have no wish to build a new clocktower.' However, this did not deter the celebrated Francis Bacon, as Lord Chancellor, from accepting bribery, for which he was fined £40,000, though King James I remitted the fine to banishment, after Bacon had pleaded that he had always acted impartially, as he had always taken bribes from both sides!

William Shakespeare must have heard the clock striking many times on his visits to Westminster, and no doubt it left a deep impression on his mind, so that we can give poetic licence to his anachronism of a clock being heard to strike in Brutus's orchard. The ancient Romans had to manage with water-clocks, sundials or candle-clocks and such similar devices. The earliest mechanical clocks originated in monastic establishment about a thousand years after Julius Caesar and were simply devices for automatically striking bells at specific times for religious observances and had neither hands nor dials.

It is probable that the mechanism for this early clock would have looked rather like a four-poster bed made of timber and iron, controlled by a primitive form of verge escapement; quite likely it had a 'foliet' – a kind of dumb-bell balance bar swinging in the horizontal plane, which preceded the vertically swinging pendulum.

The fact that it had a dial and a hand was a homage to the importance of the place of the clock on the palace, which was then not only the main royal residence but also the seat of government. At that time only a small proportion of the nobility and the clergy could read and write or understand the message of a hand upon a dial. Most of the population relied solely on the count of the hour bell.

The bell weighed 4 tons 300 pounds and was a great size for its era. Although officially called 'Edward', it was soon nicknamed 'Great Tom of Westminster', and its tones sounded through some three centuries. There is an old document which relates that in the earthquake of 1579, which caused such devastation in Westminster, the bell 'struck itself against its hammer', but both the clock and the tower apparently escaped serious damage.

At a time when few could read or write, there were very few records kept of the maintenance of the clock or bell. The scanty details which remain are mainly entries in account books of the costs of repairs or payments for the supervision of the clock, although it is not always clear whether the small amounts involved were for actual work or as an extension of royal patronage. As the years progressed, the accounts became more specific, and in the time of Henry VI the sum of 13s. 4d. was paid to one Thomas the Clockmaker for superintendence, as well as small sums for the repair of timber at the top of the tower and replacement of various items in the years 1426–8. In the time of James I, Ranulph Bull was the keeper of the Royal Clock at Westminster and did much repair work according to the entry for £56. 13s. 4d: 'delivered to him on his oath to one of the Barons of the Exchequer, without account or imprest, to be made thereof by writ dated 24th. March 1617'. The form of this record shows some of the difficulties of tracing the upkeep of even the royal timepieces at that period.

In the year 1622 Ranulph Bull's place as custodian of the Westminster Clock was taken by David Ramsey, who was to become one of the foremost horologists of his time. In 1631 he persuaded King Charles I to incorporate the Worshipful Company of Clockmakers, and duly became its first Master. This was a great step forward in the history of horology and was the foundation of the honoured craft for which Britain was to become renowned. How ironical it was that this Worshipful Company, founded by the custodian of the Westminster Clock, which did so much to establish the science and practice of clockmaking, should, some two hundred years later, take a leading role in opposition to the development of that refinement of horological science which was to produce the mechanism of Big Ben!

Great Tom of Westminster did not escape the conflicts of the Civil War. In March 1648, when King Charles I was in Cromwell's custody, a crowd of the young apprentices of the City of London clashed with the train-bands in Moorfields. These young men, as rebellious as the students of the present century, were always critical of established authority and no doubt found the strictly authoritarian rule of the Puritans very irksome. They set about the train-band, struck down their captain, captured his colours and, having armed themselves from houses they broke into, so alarmed the Lord Mayor that he fled to the Tower of London for refuge. The apprentices marched to Westminster shouting 'King Charles! King Charles!' Near the Palace they encountered sterner opponents in Lord Fairfax and a part of Cromwell's Model Army, which routed them with many casualties. But their revolt had caught on and in the next few days they were reinforced by some three hundred men from Surrey who clamoured for the release of the King.

Heavy fighting took place in New Palace Yard and, after some setbacks, the Royalists took refuge in the Great Tom clocktower, which they felt they could hold against a siege. Indeed, they put up a stout defence, and, when their gunpowder was exhausted, hurled down many of the stones and all the loose gear they could detach from the clock upon their besiegers. But eventually they had to surrender.

It appears that the damage done to the clock mechanism by the search for missiles was eventually repaired, but it was said that it was never the same again in either its accuracy or its reliability: during a famous court-martial it was claimed that the clock had struck thirteen, and this evidence was accepted by the court! In 1692 the clock was reported as being in a deplorable state, and shortly afterwards it finally ceased to function. Perhaps it was this famous clock which prompted John Dryden, who was then getting old himself, to write:

'Till like a clock, worn out with eating time,
The wheels of weary life at last stood still.

The bell, however, remained in good order but then its massive size and bulk were such that, at this age, a small battle and a short siege could do it little damage.

By 1698 the clocktower was crumbling to such an extent that it was pulled down under the directions of Sir Christopher Wren. By a grant under Privy Seal on 1 August 1698 the remains of the clocktower became the property of the Vestry of St Margaret's, Westminster (the parish church of the House of Commons), with the intent that they be sold for the benefit of the poor of the parish.

What became of the remains of the mechanism is alas unknown, but the bell, called 'Great Tom', was sold to the newly rebuilt St Paul's Cathedral for £385. 17s. 6d. There are some who have wondered whether the idea of transferring the bell to St Paul's might have influenced Christopher Wren's recommendation on the demolition of the Westminster Clock. Is it possible that the great architect coveted this famous bell for his new cathedral? Had that been the case, he must have been grieved when, in transit along the Strand *en route* to St Paul's, it fell off its carriage (at a spot still known as Bell Yard) and was shattered. It lay there for some years until funds were available to have it recast by Wrightman. Twice it was recast with unsatisfactory results, and it was not until 1716 that a satisfactory casting was made by Pheps, with some additional metal which increased its weight to five tons. The bell still retains its old name of Great Tom, but it is now 'Great Tom of St Paul's'. It has deputized for Big Ben on the radio on several occasions whilst the Great Clock has been under overhaul. It is interesting to note that the two clocks have been connected not only by the metal of the bell but also by the genius of Lord Grimthorpe, who designed both mechanisms and ensured the accuracy of both Tom and Ben by the Grimthorpe double three-legged gravity escapement.

The bell was installed in St Paul's with a Langley Bradley mechanism which continued functioning for more than two hundred years, until, after the success of Big Ben, the then Dean of St Paul's (Dean Gregory) asked Lord Grimthorpe to design a similar mechanism to replace the rather clumsy old movement. The result was a mechanism very similar to that of Big Ben, although made by John Smith & Sons of Derby, with one very important difference in that the size of the clock-room enabled the flyfans to be mounted horizontally, as was originally intended for Big Ben.

For the next 261 years New Palace Yard was destined to be without a clock. Instead in 1707 a sundial was erected near the site of the old clocktower, and on it was inscribed the same text from Virgil, 'Discite Justitiam Moniti', as was earlier around the dial of the old clock. The text was no doubt beneficial to those who stopped to read and construe, but it lacked the firm moral guidance of the hourly message from Great Tom. The fact that this message was sadly needed may be seen from the successful trials for corruption of the Earl of Macclesfield, the Lord Chancellor, and others in the eight-eenth century.

There was, adjacent to the sundial, an ancient public fountain, which on special occasions of public rejoicing was adapted to run wine instead of water. A new fountain was installed by subscription of Members to commemorate the Silver Jubilee of Queen Elizabeth II but, alas, no facilities have been incorporated to enable it to be used as a wine-dispenser.

3 The Importance of Timekeeping in Parliament

'Time Rules Everything.'
Motto chosen by Sir Harold Wilson MP
on becoming a Knight of the Garter

In the ancient world there was a concept of time very different from that of the busy life of today. Then the passing of hours, and indeed of days, counted for little. Even now in many regions, mainly in the warmer areas of the planet, the inhabitants' timekeeping is very different from that in the western world, where every second counts, and even that second is divided into thousands of millions of parts for the access time of a computer. In the thirteenth and fourteenth centuries the purpose of clocks was mainly for ensuring that religious observances were conducted at approximately the correct intervals. The king's clocks were more for prestige symbols than for efficient planning of Court life.

For many centuries the slower tempo of work in earlier Parliament meant that the pressures of time were less important. Life had fewer distractions and very much less entertainment in those days, and it was usual for Members of Parliament, like everyone else, to sit and enjoy (or sleep through) a two- to three-hour sermon every Sunday. So long speeches in the Commons were the order of the day, and time spent listening to them was rarely grudged. At that period parliamentary sittings were usually adjusted to the season of the year. In spring and summer it was quite usual to commence sittings at seven o'clock in the morning, and then to run on until the hunger of the assembled company caused them to adjourn, often for the rest of the day, to enjoy a hearty meal.

In the sixteenth and seventeenth centuries dinners were often taken between 3 and 4 p.m., and it was unusual to stay up late, even in summer.

Late sittings of Parliament were very rare. In 1621 the House of Commons did sit late by candlelight to pass a Petition of Rights to King James I, but the King tore it up, and also the extracts from the Journal of the House (whose mutilated pages can still be seen in the library); the grounds for the rejection was that it was 'passed at an unreasonable hour of the day'. Eight o'clock in the evening, when this was passed, would now be considered an unusually early hour today.

With the increase in parliamentary business due to a growing economy and colonial possessions in the eighteenth and nineteenth centuries, time became of vastly greater importance and it became essential for every entry into the records of Parliament to be noted with the actual time not only of the start and finish of each debate but also of the beginning and end of every speech made by a Member. Furthermore a detailed timing had to be kept of every Instrument and every paper placed upon the Table of the House. The Clerks of the House have the particular duty to keep a precise record of the time of every occurrence. Contrary to general belief, these clerks keep no record of what is said in the speeches (that later became the responsibility of Hansard, although it is all now tape-recorded): their task is to record all occurrences with their precise times, the tally of votes cast, the Bills passed and the Acts receiving Royal Assent.

Although the House of Commons, on an average, sits for some 1,700 hours every year (more than twice the sitting time of any other parliament in the world), there is never enough parliamentary time to consider all the motions, bills and other measures put forward by the Government, the Opposition and the Backbenchers. The result is that many worthy motions and resolutions have to be 'talked out' for lack of time. In the same way the very important Prime Minister's Question Time has to be limited to fifteen minutes, and any questions not reached in that time can only receive written replies – which rules out the all-important 'supplementaries' which are so often the crux of the question.

It is thus most important that Members be kept aware

continually of the accurate time not only in the debating chamber but throughout the Palace. Although the chimes of Big Ben can be clearly heard within the Chamber of the Commons, it is not sufficient for Members to be reminded of the time only every quarter of an hour, and so there must be accurate clocks both in the Debating Chambers and throughout the Palace, for minute-by-minute timing.

The great importance of accurate timing in the House of Commons was heavily underlined when there was once the danger of Members being deprived of the exact time due to a strike. In May 1975 the manual workers unions of the Civil Service called a strike to support their demands for a higher pay settlement. Some of the union leaders hoped that, by depriving Members of heating and other facilities, they would be able to close down Parliament and so put pressure on the Government (Labour at that time) to agree to their demands. The manual workers in the Palace did not wish to strike and told their unions that they were not going to take part. The unions, however, refused to accept their refusal and told them in no uncertain terms that they had got to strike and to raise picket lines near the entrances to the building. One of these picket lines near the entrance adjacent to Big Ben had a large notice: 'LIKE BIG BEN WE HAVE GOT TO STRIKE.' In the middle of the strike there was the usual change over to Summer Time, and the Resident Engineer told the pickets that he was going to stop Big Ben striking for four hours whilst he changed the hour – and wouldn't they stop striking too? They saw the point but were too much in the power of the unions to be able to respond.

By taking emergency measures, it was possible to keep the heating and all the engineering services and facilities functioning, but although Big Ben was showing correct time, there was a problem concerning the thousand other clocks which were normally regulated by the visiting clockman of the Department of the Environment, who as a loyal union member was on strike. The electric clocks all continued working normally but, with the change to Summer Time, showed an hour behind. This could easily have been corrected by a small adjustment in the Engineering Control Room, but this was forbidden by the Civil Service authorities, who feared that it would spread the strike. The Commons, however, felt it absolutely essential for the conduct of vital parliamentary business to have accurate clocks showing the correct time in their Chamber. To cover an emergency there were some large battery-driven clocks in store, and the Resident Engineer proposed installing these, but in the face of union objections it was necessary for him to go to the highest levels of the Civil Service before permission was granted. The clocks were started at the correct time and hung on loops of cord before the faces of the existing clocks so that the business of the House could proceed. This incident served to illustrate how vital the display of the accurate time is to the conduct of the nation's business in Parliament.

Time is the most powerful weapon in the hands of Her Majesty's Opposition and is very skilfully used by all political parties. Whilst governments use the limitations of time to prevent detailed discussions of matters they do not like, oppositions try to prolong the debates in the hope that they will run out of time or get 'talked out'. Frequently governments will suggest that matters which the opposition feel very strongly about should be brought up on a 'Supply Day' when the opposition has the choice of subjects to debate. This manoeuvre frequently puts the opposition in the cleft stick of deciding how best the limited time of a Supply Day can be employed. It is possible for a Member to bring up a motion under the 'Ten Minute Rule' and talk about it for that length of time, but such a motion will never get any further unless the government decides to incorporate it into their existing plans for legislation. There is also a scheme for 'Early Day Motions', some hundred of which are listed on every Order Paper for possible debate when proceedings finish unusually early. In fact, it is universally recognized that time never permits such debates to occur, and most of such motions are inserted for their publicity value and in the hope of gaining parliamentary support.

One of the measures which many think would lead to more effective use of time in the Commons would be a limitation on the length of speeches. This has never received effective support, although efforts to control persist to the present time. A reason for this lack of success is that it flies in the face of the long traditions of the great orators of preceding centuries. Also it has been found useful by both government and opposition. This lack of time restriction, however, inevitably leads to the government, anxious to get through an important measure, imposing the 'Guillotine', a measure for terminating discussion on a bill on a predetermined date; this is heartily disliked by both government and opposition as it usually leaves a number of clauses which have never been reached. Use of the guillotine always throw much extra work on the House of Lords, which has to combine with its normal duties as a revising Chamber the added responsibility of voicing the views of the opposition on those clauses not previously debated.

The House of Lords, which is second only to the Commons on the duration of annual sittings among the world's parliaments, has also had its problems on length of speeches but has solved it in characteristic style. Before a bill is received from the Commons, they have a brief meeting and decide the time which will be made available for its consideration on the floor of the House. If it is decided that five hours should be devoted to debate, they might say, 'We will allow thirty-five minutes for the opening speeches and twenty-five minutes for the closing ones. That leaves about three hours for other speeches, and as eighteen peers have indicated they would like to speak, that would mean we would ask them to limit their time to ten minutes each.' To measure the time taken and to guide peers whilst on their feet, special digital elapsed time clocks are installed, visible to everyone, which are started when the peer rises and display the length of the contribution. There are no penalties for overrunning the allotted time but in the House of Lords this arrangement has been most effective.

The importance of time increased only slowly over the centuries. Early Parliaments had been able to meet the needs of the period for some 150 years without a great clock or any very accurate timepiece. But when it became necessary to rebuild the Palace of Westminster, the greater pressures of time were becoming apparent.

4   The Idea of a New Great Clock

Eternity is in love with the productions of time.
William Blake, *Proverbs of Hell*

On the night of 16 October 1834 the greater part of the ancient Palace of Westminster was destroyed by a fire which consumed both Houses of Parliament.

The cause of the fire came from the burning of vast quantities of Exchequer tallies in the furnace under the House of Lords. The tallies, which had survived from the Middle Ages, when there was a great shortage of coins, were in the form of wooden strips, made in two parts which had to 'tally' (fit into each other) and which were commonly used for currency up to the nineteenth century. They were finally declared illegal in 1826, but it took a long time to withdraw them to the Exchequer, then within the Palace of Westminster, which soon became overloaded, and it was decided to burn them. The two workmen detailed to do the burning overloaded the furnaces and left them to burn. With the flues partly blocked, the fire spread to the store of tallies, and with a strong south-western wind the flames engulfed the Palace.

Parliament was prorogued until the New Year whilst temporary accommodation was provided for the House of Commons in the repaired Court of Requests, which in olden days had been the banqueting hall of the old Palace and before the fire had been the Lords Chamber. The House of Lords was fitted into the old Painted Chamber, traditionally the bedchamber of Edward the Confessor.

The old buildings, which had evolved with little planning from what had been the principal royal residence, were cramped, stuffy and inconvenient. Members had pressed for years for the erection of a new and more spacious building more suitable for the larger role Parliament was playing in a great industrial nation. A Select Committee of the Commons was formed to consider the rebuilding of the Palace and in due course issued an open invitation to architects to enter a competition for the design of a new palace in either Gothic or Elizabethan style, to harmonize with the ancient Westminster Hall (saved from the fire) and with the adjacent Westminster Abbey.

The Commissioners examined ninety-four entries, none of which featured a clocktower as the most prominent feature of the building at that stage. After much deliberation they selected Design No. 64, by Charles Barry, and details of the proposed building were discussed at great length. Following these discussions and further collaboration between Charles Barry and Augustus Welby Pugin, his very gifted assistant, revised façades were presented to a joint Committee of Lords and Commons on 22 April 1836 which featured a clock on the northern tower surmounted by a spire. This scheme was approved by the Commissioners on 28 April 1836.

There is a story that on the night of the fire Charles Barry, then a promising young architect, was travelling into London from the south and stopped his coach on a hill to look down on the great blaze, perhaps wondering if there would be the possible opportunity of being personally involved in the building of a replacement Houses of Parliament.

His final designs incorporated a very fine clocktower (although somewhat lower than the one eventually built) with four dials, each thirty feet in diameter. The clock was to have a fourteen-ton hour bell and eight quarter bells. The clock-tower was to be situated near where that of Great Tom had stood and was to be surmounted by a beautiful spire to conform with the requirement that the overall building style of the building should be Gothic, and to provide a contrast with the planned Victoria Tower on the south side of the Palace. This was not quite the end of the matter as, following the exhibition of the designs of the proposed elevations of the building at the Royal Academy in 1844, there was criticism of the provision of a clocktower by some Members who were concerned at the increase in cost and who suggested that there was no need of a public clock. However, the general feeling was that the beauty and dignity of this building would be enhanced by a worthy clocktower.

The Office of Works had already laid down that there should be 'A Noble Clock, a King among Clocks' but had left it like that, with no further instructions for the next eight years. Perhaps the Office was taking the line laid down by its First Commissioner at that time, Lord Lincoln (later fifth Duke of Newcastle), who always maintained that it was best to let the expert have a free hand to get on with the job, since he knows more about it than any minister or civil servant. Unfortunately, in this case, he had omitted to appoint an expert.

As the construction of the tower was progressing, Charles Barry, having received no specific instructions, considered that the provision of the clock had been left to him in much the same way as a church clock was often left to the architect to arrange. He did not consider that, as this was to be the largest and most important clock in the world at that time, it might be wise to get scientific advice from an expert. Perhaps at that period he did not think there were any horological experts apart from the clock-manufacturers. After getting formal approval from the Office of Works, he wrote to Louis Vulliamy, Clockmaker to the Queen, asking him for his terms for the design of a great clock and if there would be an extra price if he was not subsequently asked to manufacture and install the clock. Needless to say, this caused something of a stir in the clockmaking world, and many very good manufacturers felt it unfair that this great opportunity should go to one firm without competition.

This was especially felt by those firms that had pioneered the development of the chronometer which was the super-accurate timepiece of extreme reliability developed for navigation and which had earned Britain the reputation of being the best precision clockmaker in the world (see also page 104). They considered that it would be wrong for the greatest clock in the world to be made as a single tender by a famous clockmaker who they considered to be old-fashioned and whose designs reflected none of the unique maritime experience which had been built up in this country over the last half century.

One of these manufacturers, Edward John Dent, who had

Inside one of the great dials

Mechanism of the great clock

Method of making the bell mould

The bell is taken to Westminster

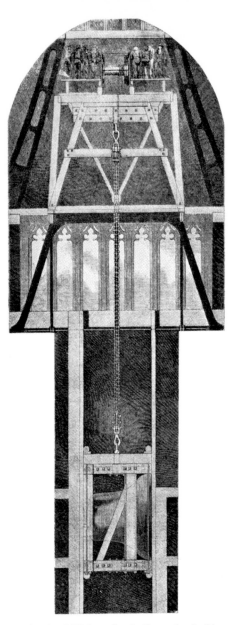

Method of lifting the bell to the belfry

The bell and hammer set up experimentally in New Palace Yard

E. J. Dent

Lord Grimthorpe (E.B. Denison QC)

Sir George Airy

Pennies on the pendulum

Crack in Big Ben II

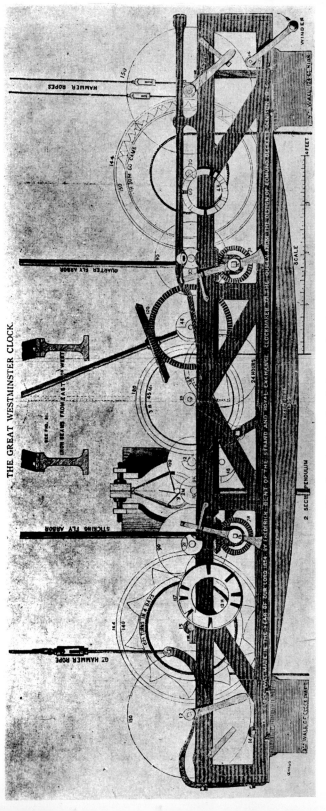

Denison's sketch of the mechanism

also just completed a very accurate public clock for the Royal Exchange, wrote to the Astronomer Royal, with whom he had been involved in the perfection of the chronometer, to ask him for a testimonial to assist him in seeking an opportunity to tender for the design and construction of the new clock. The Astronomer Royal, who had found Dent one of the most enterprising chronometer-makers and the recipient of several awards, was pleased to assist and wrote to the First Commissioner of Woods and Works, at that time Viscount Canning.

The result of that letter was a request from Canning that the Astronomer Royal be referee for the Great Clock, saying, 'It is of importance that the clock which is to be placed in the clocktower of the New Houses of Parliament should be the very best which British science and skill can supply.' So the idea of a Great Clock, which would be not only the biggest but also the best in the world was finally fully established some ten years after the fire which had destroyed the old Palace. This idea was, however, still far from the end of the matter, as the decision to appoint the Astronomer Royal as referee generated strong feelings in the Worshipful Company of Clockmakers, of which Louis Vulliamy was Master, and started great controversies. Big Ben was not destined to be completed for a further period of fifteen strife-torn years.

5 The Early Conflicts

The time is out of joint; O cursed spite,
That ever I was born to set it right!
Shakespeare, *Hamlet*

Even the legendary God Chronos, Father of Zeus and Master
of Time, who formed the world from Chaos, would have been
appalled by the utter chaos and deep personal animosities
aroused by the creation of what has become the most famous
timepiece in the world. Although the sounds of the great bells
are redolent of peace and stability, the history of the construction of the clock and bells engendered some of the bitterest
public controversy ever known up to that time. This controversy was often conducted through letters to the great
newspapers of the day, and the language was often intemper-
ate and sometimes even downright abusive, leading to the
exchange of writs and to long legal battles.

This was most unfortunate, as the protagonists were all
basically devoted, well-meaning men of spotless integrity,
with the public interest very much at heart. They were also
men who had endured difficult lives with constant struggles to
achieve their very worthy ends, in the face of many frustra-
tions. None of them would ever have reached such heights of
achievement if they had had easy personalities for working
together, and their clashes of opinions often brought out their
sharp tempers and the very worst of all their characteristics.
This was a time of great discoveries and inventions in science,
engineering and architecture, and the applications of new
materials, ideas and technologies were bound to arouse disagreements and even conflicts. Furthermore the interven-
tions of lords, civil servants and often ill-informed politicians
were very frustrating.

Mr (later Sir) Charles Barry, the architect of the new Palace, was the genius able to transform the ill-shaped and difficult site into what has been described as one of the wonders of the world. He was also a practical and flexible man, open to new ideas and techniques and able to accept the clothing of his basic ideal of a classical building, internally and externally with Gothic façades, designed with the wonderful collaboration of the greatest master of the neo-Gothic style, Augustus Welby Pugin. He showed his flexibility in the use of a cast-iron framework for the Palace, and in his mass-production methods, which, combined with the use of an overhead travelling steam-crane, were well ahead of his age.

Barry had many difficulties with the Committees of the Houses, who were always trying to change his designs, and with the Prince Consort's Committee for the Interior Decoration of the Palace, on which, strangely enough, he was not represented. Furthermore, to add to his difficulties, without consulting him a Dr Reid, a man noted for his strong opinions and passionate temper, was appointed Heating, Lighting and Ventilation Engineer, with authority to do work and to demand vast spaces for airways, plant rooms and ducts etc outside the control of the architect. This extra burden was enough to try the patience of a saint – and Barry was no saint!

To Barry the provision of even the Great Clock must have seemed a very minor matter and, having had no specific instructions from the Office of Woods and Works, he gained their approval to call in Louis Vulliamy, whose son had worked for Barry, to draw up an acceptable design. The fact that this cosy arrangement was afterwards overruled would have made for somewhat difficult arrangements between clock designer and architect, even if the transition has not been accompanied by a serious personal attack. As it was, the necessary co-operation on all the building requirement was almost non-existent, and there were public criticisms from each side at every stage of the project.

Louis Vulliamy was a renowned clockmaker of the old school, who had made clocks of many kinds and sizes and was credited with the introduction of the two-second pendulum into England. He was highly regarded in his profession and was Master of the Worshipful Company of Clockmakers for many years. He was Clockmaker to the Queen, responsible for the care of all the clocks in Buckingham Palace up to the day of his death. He had produced a wide range of high quality clocks of most excellent design and workmanship which still keep good time and which are ornaments to many of the greatest palaces, homes and clubs in the world. To him a turret clock was a first-class mechanism which would keep time to reasonable limits but could not, of course, be compared for accuracy or reliability with the chronometers which had been brought to a high standard of perfection in the preceding decades, to enable mariners to tell their longitude. He frequently drew attention to the great difference between a chronometer, with its tiny movement and diminutive hands, and the great mechanism of a turret clock, which had to move four sets of very large hands in all conditions of snow, rain and high winds.

Vulliamy was delighted to receive the commission to prepare the design, specification and drawings for the Great Clock, which he estimated would take two years to prepare and would cost 100 guineas on the basis that, if he were not entrusted with the construction of the clock, he would be paid a further 100 guineas. He also let it be known that, in his position in the profession, he did not prepare tenders or compete with other clockmakers. After discussion with the Office of Woods and Works, this was accepted by Barry on 26 April 1944.

Edward John Dent, also Clockmaker to the Queen, had made a wide range of clocks as well as doing much innovatory work on the perfection of the chronometer. He had been granted the First Premium Award for Marine Chronometers in 1829 and had followed this by showing that chronometers need not be considered intricate laboratory instruments, each separately made painstakingly by hand, but could be systematically manufactured in bulk, with a great saving in cost which enabled them to be fitted to a larger number of ships.

Dent had recently completed a large turret clock for the Royal Exchange and felt that, with his wide expertise, he could compete for the construction of the Great Clock. Having enjoyed good relations with the Astronomer Royal on the improvement of the chronometer, he wrote to him asking for a testimonial to forward to the Chief Commissioner with his application to tender for the design and construction.

Mr (later Sir) George Airy, the Astronomer Royal, was a brilliant scientist who in his younger days had been a Senior Wrangler and, in 1823, a Smith's Prizeman. He had first-rate theoretical knowledge of timekeeping and some practical experience in the trials of the new chronometers, which had put his Greenwich Observatory on the map of the world. He was, perhaps, too advanced in his views on the application of scientific principles and developments for the majority of old-fashioned clockmakers, with whom he had had a number of serious disagreements even before 1844. He regarded Dent as one of the most enlightened clockmakers of the age and was pleased to give him a glowing testimonial. When the Chief Commissioner wrote to Airy on 22 June 1844 asking him to act as referee for the design and construction of the Great Clock, it brought an enthusiastic reply the same month.

When Airy accepted the task he gave a full and detailed specification of fifteen conditions of the fundamental criteria required for the construction of the clock (see Appendix I). He further advised that he considered E. J. Dent & Co the most suitable firm to construct the clock, but if three tenders were essential, he suggested that Louis Vulliamy and Whitehurst of Derby be invited to tender.

John Whitehurst had founded the firm of Whitehurst of Derby in 1736 to make turret clocks of exceptional quality. He was one of the first makers to incorporate temperature compensation into his pendulums by the use of a bimetallic rod of his own design. He was also the originator of the 'tell-tale' clocks used by watchmen and the first time-recorders. He was made a Fellow of the Royal Society in 1779, after which he moved to London and engaged on more philosophical studies. His son John Whitehurst II continued making high-grade clocks until his death in 1834. John Whitehurst III, the grandson of the founder, was less interested and the business gradually decayed until, when his health failed, he sold it to William Roskill of Liverpool. This did not stop the gradual decay, and the firm was soon wound up.

The Astronomer Royal's advice was taken and Charles Barry was duly instructed to send out invitations to the three firms to tender, incorporating the Astronomer Royal's specification. In doing so, Barry felt strongly that this late decision had undermined his previous action. His reaction was mild, however, compared with that of Vulliamy, who fairly exploded with indignation and wrath. He did not pause to consider that he was being paid 100 guineas or more for the work the other two firms were to provide without any payment. He objected to the choice of the Astronomer Royal as the referee and declared that it was quite impossible to construct a clock of this size that could meet the specification as far as the requirements for accuracy demanded. He further declared that, on principle, he never undertook designs or commissions in competition with others, and furthermore it was quite impossible to estimate the cost of such a clock. He also took outside action by urging the Clockmakers Company and others in the industry to protest that the specification was unworkable. He pressed the point that it was quite different making an accurate chronometer from constructing a Great Clock, where the hands and mechanism weighed many tons and where the effects of wind and weather had to be considered. At his bidding, the Worshipful Company of Clockmakers addressed a memorial to Parliament to ask for less severe conditions, but this received scant attention.

The other two firms accepted the specification, and the first tender was received from Dent in the sum of £1,500 on 8 August 1846, whilst Whitehurst sent in his tender for £3,373 on 24 September 1846. On 29 August 1846 Vulliamy sent in his drawings and specification (to earn his commission fee) but sent no tender price. (Many years later Vulliamy wrote in a letter to the Office that his price would have been about £3,500.) Airy had correspondence with both Dent and Whitehurst, and added an extra condition to his list of fifteen which required the addition of an electro-mechanical device to generate a signal for the regulation of other clocks in the Palace. Dent required an extra £100 for this facility, making his total £1,600, and Whitehurst an extra £150, making his total £3,523.

On 18 May 1847 Airy sent his report to the First Commissioner, in which he made no specific recommendations on acceptance of either tender but left the choice to the Commissioner. However, he indicated, after visiting both factories, that Dent had the more efficient organization as well as the cheaper price and, through a better system of working, had previously reduced the price of chronometers materially. Commenting on Vulliamy's design, with no price, the Astronomer Royal wrote: 'I have very carefully examined Mr Vulliamy's beautiful plans. In regard to the provisions for strength, solidity, power and general largeness of dimensions, they are excellent. In regard to delicacy they fail: and they fail so much, that I think myself justified in saying that such a clock would be a village clock of a very superior character, but would not have the accuracy of an astronomical clock.'

Although this letter was sent out in May 1847, no action was taken by the Office of Woods and Works. The Astronomer Royal's comments on his design, however, came to the notice of Vulliamy, who then stated that he was willing to submit his design and prices to a committee of the members of the Company of Clockmakers. He further declared that the clocks offered by his competitors could never be made to the accuracies demanded by the Astronomer Royal. As it was recognized at the time that Vulliamy was the mainspring of the Company of Clockmakers, this offer was not considered very advantageous. In particular it was felt, by all concerned, that the great clock on the new Houses of Parliament should be not only the biggest but also the best in the world. To this end it was most desirable that the latest scientific advice, based on the great step forward in navigation by the chronometer developed under the guidance of successive Astronomers Royal, should be fully utilized.

At this stage in the controversy there was an occurrence which caused concern to all those involved. In 1845 Dent had been promised, as an inducement for his unpaid work in the design and tendering for the Great Clock, the opportunity to tender for all the hundreds of other clocks in the Palace of Westminster. In the spring of 1847, having received no invitations to tender, he made a number of enquiries and found that Barry was ordering all these clocks directly from Vulliamy. He sent several letters of complaint to the Office of Woods and Works, reminding them of their undertaking, without any visible results, whilst the orders to Vulliamy continued. As his letters did not appear to be having the desired effect, Dent took the drastic step of withdrawing his tender for the Great Clock on 3 July 1847. He also wrote to the Astronomer Royal

explaining his action. Airy contacted the Chief Commissioner, and there was a considerable rumpus at the Office. It was
then said that, due to an oversight, Barry had never been told
of the undertaking which had been given, or of the desirability of seeking separate quotations in competition for the work
he was putting out. On the receipt of full and firm assurances
that no more clocks would be ordered without his firm being
given an opportunity to tender, Dent wrote a letter on 4
August 1847 from St Petersburg (where he was advising on
the Tsar's clocks) asking to be allowed to remain a competi-
tor. This was agreed by the Office of Woods and Works on 20
August 1847.

No account of the controversies around the building of this
famous clock could possibly overlook the influences of the
political head of the government department responsible for
the construction of the new Palace of Westminster and his
civil servants. At the commencement of the project the
department was known as the Office of Woods and Forests,
but over the years there were several changes in name,
although little in general characteristics, and to simplify the
story it is easiest to refer to as the Office of Works, which is
the title by which it was best known over the last century.
Over the years of controversy and indecision there were many
holders of the political post of First Commissioner, and
although most of them were in office for a very short time
(with a high turnover of peers), they had a great influence in
the decisions made in their name. The major figures were as
follows:

Lord Lincoln (later Duke of Newcastle) 1841–6. A First
Commissioner who was strongly in favour of a very fine clock
for the new palace, but firmly believed in leaving the design
and details to experts – without appointing an expert!

Viscount Canning had only a part of 1846 in office but in
that period appointed the Astronomer Royal as referee for
the clock.

Lord Morpeth (later Earl of Carlisle) was in office 1846–50
at a time of austerity in public finance and ordered that all
work of an ornamental nature was to be postponed. This, no
doubt, had some effect on the delay in letting the contract for
the clock over these years. He appointed Denison joint
referee with the Astronomer Royal.

Lord Seymour (later Duke of Somerset), 1850–1 paved the way for the letting of the contract for the clock in January 1852.

Lord John Manners (later Duke of Rutland) served for only a few months in 1852 but was again First Commissioner 1858–9. Considered by some the least helpful Commissioner.

Sir William Molesworth, 1852–5 was an aristocratic radical who was much swayed by his civil servants. Their very strong antipathy to Denison resulted in his resignation in 1855.

Sir Benjamin Hall, 1855–8, was an adept and capable politician, with a charming manner, who quickly persuaded Denison to withdraw his resignation and resume his duties. He did much to help to further the Great Clock, and it is appropriate that his name should be linked with the nickname of Big Ben.

Henry Fitzroy MP, 1859, was in office only for a few months before his early death.

William Cowper MP (stepson of Lord Palmerston), 1860–66, complained that Big Ben's 'loud and dismal tones' drowned ministers' voices in the Commons Chamber, a complaint which, strangely enough, did not receive much support from the House.

The civil servants of the Office were not, of course, expected to know anything about clocks, and unfortunately they had no one to advise them except the Astronomer Royal, with whom they were not always in tune. Alexander Milne, Secretary in the time of Lord Lincoln and Viscount Canning, was happy to work with the Astronomer Royal's advice, but his successor, T. W. Phillips, was of a different mind. He was Secretary throughout most of the period of the bitterest controversy and appears to have had antipathy for the Astronomer Royal. This strong feeling appears also to have been carried forward to both Denison and Dent, possibly because they were favoured by Airy, which meant that every possible difficulty and disturbance was magnified by his handling. An example of his animosity was when, without any consultation, he invited Robert Stevenson, the famous railway engineer, who had no horological experience, to join Airy and Denison as referees for the Great Clock. When it was apparent that both Airy and Denison would resign, he dropped Stevenson without further explanation.

The entry of Edmund Beckett Denison QC into the controversy came about a year after the Astronomer Royal and the Commissioners had expressed their complete satisfaction with the tenders received but had made no move to proceed further with the letting of the necessary contract for construction. This may have been due to normal bureaucratic delay in the Office or to financial stringency. Whichever it was, it caused strong feelings among many, among them Denison (the son of a Member of Parliament and himself, at a later stage, Leader of the Parliamentary Bar). He was a strange and complex character of great genius, in the course of a long and varied career known by three names: Edmund Beckett Denison was the name by which he was christened; he became Sir Edmund Beckett when he inherited a baronetcy on condition that he amend his name accordingly; and in later life he was elevated to the peerage as Lord Grimthorpe. For the period of the construction of the Great Clock he was known as Denison, and this name will be used as it is inscribed in letters of iron along the bedplate of Big Ben.

Although he was an eminent barrister, Denison was also a mathematician who had made an extensive study of clock-making and had written the section on clocks in the *Encyclopaedia Britannica*. At this time he was writing *A Rudimentary Treatise on Clocks, Watches & Bells*, first published in 1850 and still in print today, still regarded as an authoritative work on the subject. This was the age of the gifted amateur who could turn his hand to a wide variety of disciplines with outstanding success, and Denison had also a great interest in Gothic architecture and was known to have been somewhat critical of some of Barry's work. He was in later life (1879) to re-design and restore a large part of St Albans Abbey, a project which also attracted a measure of public controversy, the echoes of which still sound today. He was well known for his strong opinions and most aggressive manner, and the brilliance which ensured that he was so often right in his opinions did little to make him popular with his contemporaries.

Denison was indeed a genius, gifted, resourceful and energetic, but at the same time unscrupulous, mischievous and opinionated, willing to go to any length to justify and substantiate his ideas and prejudices. His unusual determination and forceful drive were just what the Great Clock needed at that time. Unfortunately he had no diplomacy and never considered the feelings of others, which made him extremely difficult to work with on any project.

The occasion of Denison's entry into the great task, in which he was destined to play the major role, arose from a letter he sent to the First Commissioner, Viscount Morpeth, in May 1848, in which he drew attention to the unbelievable delays that had already occurred in the provision of the clock. It was, perhaps, an inauspicious entry into the matter, as he virtually accused Barry of preventing the clock being ordered because Viscount Canning had prevented his placing it with Vulliamy. This was unjust, as the delay was largely in the Office of Works, although Barry did nothing to expedite their action on the matter. It also boded ill for future relations with the architect. However, it did draw attention, at the highest level, to the very slow progress of the provision of the clock, and resulted in Viscount Morpeth, after consultation with the Astronomer Royal, appointing Denison joint referee with Airy. This was indeed a major step forward in the building of the clock because, although Airy was a gifted scientist, he lacked the drive and determination which Denison could and did provide.

Denison took his duties very seriously and immediately engaged on a full examination of Dent's design, with many suggestions for improvements which virtually constituted a complete re-design. This re-design was not, however, permitted to increase the price already submitted, as it was estimated that, even if there was a small loss on the contract, it would soon be offset by the extra business brought to the firm by this prestigious order. This was a very good collaboration, with Denison's theoretical knowledge complementing Dent's practical experience and initiative, and the two very different men became friends.

After making a full examination of all three designs, Denison wrote to the First Commissioner as follows: 'I believe few people have paid more attention to the subject of turret clocks than I have; and I have employed both Dent and Vulliamy to make church clocks for friends who have consulted me. I have no hesitation in saying that I consider Dent's work of that sort very superior to Vulliamy's, as Vulliamy's is to that of most other makers; and there is less comparison, in my opinion, between their scientific knowledge and ingenuity . . .' Unfortunately for future relations between Denison and Barry, he concluded the letter with the comment: 'It is impossible not to feel that he [Dent] is under a disadvantage in having the architect opposed to him and evidently doing what he can to prevent him being employed.'

Such comments in an official letter to the First Commissioner (which Phillips would have brought to Barry's attention) were to have a profound effect in steaming up the difficult relationship between the architect and the clockmaker, where close and friendly co-operation was so essential. It was also to play a part in the reconsideration of the clock design, which was to be a major cause of the great catastrophe 125 years later.

The powerful alliance of Airy, Denison and Dent did not, however, completely offset the strong hostility still maintained by the rather old-fashioned Worshipful Company of Clockmakers, which continued to maintain, through Vulliamy, that Dent's clock would never be made and that the conditions of accuracy set by Airy were impossible to achieve on a large turret clock. Vulliamy also suggested to Phillips that, as Dent had won first prize at the Great Exhibition for a turret clock, made to Denison's design, their association should be considered such as to preclude Dent from the competition for the Great Clock. Phillips supported this suggestion but withdrew in the face of a strong stand from Airy and Denison. (Incidentally, Denison was Chairman of the Horological Judges of the Great Exhibition but did not vote on this issue. The clock in question was installed on top of King's Cross Station in London, where it worked for over a hundred years before the movement was replaced by a simple electric drive in 1965.)

Even the powerful influences which Denison brought to bear on the project did not ensure that the contract was finally let until January 1852, by which time Whitehurst was dead and Dent's was the only tender. At this stage another long-established firm, Thwaites & Reed, who had constructed the clock on Westminster Abbey, asked if they could put forward a tender. The Commissioners, however, decided that, in view of the time which had passed, this was not appropriate. This seemed unfortunate to Thwaites & Reed at the time, but it was perhaps wise as at the time they lacked the genius of Dent, and perhaps Denison would not have helped them to the same extent in the design. The turn of Thwaites & Reed to help Big Ben was to come more than a century later.

Work on the construction of the mechanism started as soon as the contract was let in January 1852 and, with close collaboration and supervision from Denison, was very well advanced by 8 March 1853, when Edward John Dent died. In the normal run of affairs this would not have been of much consequence, as most of the crucial design decisions had already been taken, but the Worshipful Company of Clockmakers, under pressure from Vulliamy, represented to Phillips at the Office of Works that Frederick Rippon would be unable to complete the clock, which, in any case, they had always contended could never be built to the specification laid down by the Astronomer Royal. (Frederick Rippon was the son-in-law of E. J. Dent, who had always helped him to run the business. Under the terms of Dent's will he inherited the business on condition that he changed his name to Frederick Dent.)

In the usual way this would have been settled by the joint referees, and both the Astronomer Royal and Denison were convinced that Frederick Dent could undertake the completion and commissioning of the clock. Phillips, however, insisted on taking the matter to the Office of Works' solicitor, John Gardiner, to obtain a ruling from the Law Officers of the Crown as to whether the contract was still valid. It is puzzling to speculate why he did this, as little profit would the Office or the country gain from breaking a contract when the mechanism was half finished. There could be no question of handing over the mechanism to Vulliamy or any member of the Clockmakers Company for completion, as they had repeatedly stated that this clock could never be built! The only alternative would have been to start afresh, and this would have involved big losses.

Whatever the reasons for the referral, the ruling given by the Law Officers of the Crown, A. E. Cockburn, R. Bethell and J. S. Willis on 27 October 1853 was as follows: 'We are of the opinion that the Commissioners of Her Majesty's Works are not bound to accept the clock in question as it was not completed by the late Mr Dent and that no person who may succeed him in his business can claim to complete it for the Commissioners.'

This action by Phillips was quite unknown to Airy and Denison and even, it is believed, to the First Commissioner. It was first heard of when a letter was sent to Frederick Dent on 15 November 1853, eight months after the death of E. J. Dent, telling him that he had no contract! Had Denison known of the steps being taken to explore the legal implications of the change in the company, he would undoubtedly have taken strong preventative action, and his keen legal mind, which was to make him Leader of the Parliamentary Bar, would have found loopholes which would have amended this ruling. As it was, Dent's had done eight months work on the clock mechanism over a period when the firm had not been informed that there was any doubt about their contract. The work on the mechanism was by then approaching completion, so Frederick Dent wrote to the Office of Works, relating this position and protesting strongly at the way in which he had been treated. He also cited the fact that on 18 June 1853 Denison had had an interview with the First Commissioner (Sir William Molesworth) in which he had been asked when the mechanism would be completed, with no suggestion that the contract was or was about to be terminated.

At the end of 1853 there was the absurdly complex position of Frederick Dent having an almost completed clock mechanism with no contract or any method of obtaining payment. The Office of Works was in an equally complicated position. Phillips had got rid of Dent but had no visible alternative. He could not even get advice from Vulliamy, who was then a dying man and did in fact expire in January 1854. One cannot feel other than deep sympathy for this old man who had created some magnificent clocks in his day, which still ornament many of the greatest establishments of the world. He was the acknowledged leader of his profession when Barry approached him about the Great Clock. It was sad that he and the Worshipful Company, which he led, should have felt that they had to oppose the introduction by the innovators, who had perfected the chronometer, of new standards of accuracy into other clocks by the adoption of engineering principles. It was this that led to the Astronomer Royal's remarks on Vulliamy's Great Clock drawings which he deemed deeply insulting and which so embittered his final years.

To add to the complications of the situation, a further dispute had arisen between Denison and Barry over the space available in the clocktower. Denison claimed that Barry would not say what alterations he was making to the design of the tower; Barry maintained (correctly) that Denison would not give him full and final drawings of the mechanism. Both had good reasons for this, no doubt, but it was unfortunate that their mutual feelings of antagonism were so soured that there was no possibility of the compromises which were so necessary. Airy pleaded with Denison to give Barry what he wanted, but Denison stood his ground and said he would provide the full information only if Barry would write and say exactly what he wanted and why he needed it. It is possible that Denison did not wish to give detailed drawings of the mechanism because he feared premature disclosure before he finalized the details following accuracy tests.

The Astronomer Royal was profoundly concerned that Denison should have taken this attitude and replied that their association could not continue. There had been several other small matters on which there had been minor disagreements. Airy had put forward a number of theoretical suggestions, some of which had been accepted but many of which were not practicable. The most outstanding of these was a proposed re-alignment of the gearing in which, by error, Airy showed the shaft of one set of wheels passing through the spokes of another gearwheel. It is feared that Denison did not deal with this little mistake as diplomatically as the circumstances demanded.

On receipt of Denison's letter of 3 November 1853, giving the conditions on which he would supply the information to Barry, the Astronomer Royal wrote to the First Commissioner relinquishing his charge as a referee for the building of the Great Clock.

The First Commissioner (Sir William Molesworth) had an interview with the Astronomer Royal and persuaded him that these matters could be ironed out without his resignation. Airy, who was still profoundly interested in the Great Clock, allowed himself to be talked round and agreed to continue his duties.

In the meanwhile Denison wrote to Phillips asking him to obtain from Barry the information he required on the clock-room. Phillips was not disposed to be helpful and replied that he could not act on the request of one referee alone, only on joint action from both working together. Denison, who had not been informed that Airy had withdrawn his resignation, replied that he had no intention of not fulfilling his full responsibilities and that he had therefore given written instructions to Frederick Dent to proceed with the work on the basis of the information available, on his own authority. He added that, if expensive alterations had subsequently to be made due to lack of co-operation from Barry or the Office, 'I think Parliament and the public will have little difficulty in deciding which of the various parties are to blame for the failure, and which are not.'

It was only after this strong letter of March 1854 from so formidable a person that Phillips decided to send Frederick Dent's letter of November 1853, which had prompted no action for four months, together with the information on the action Denison had taken, to the Law Officers of the Crown for their reconsideration in the light of the further developments.

The mechanism of the clock was virtually complete in July 1854 when the Law Officers completed their reconsideration of the case and produced the following ruling: 'We are of the opinion that the facts stated by Mr Dent in his letter of the 18th November 1853, do not alter the legal bearings of the case, but we think that they make all the difference as to the course the Commissioners ought to pursue. As it appears that ever since his father's death until the time of our former opinion being taken, Mr Dent was dealt with as the party whose business it was to complete the clock, and he went on working at completion with the full knowledge of the Board and its officers. Under these circumstances, as there is no question as to Mr Dent's perfect capacity to complete it satisfactorily, we think that he should be allowed to finish it.'

Thus with the full agreement of the two referees the contractual position was finally settled, just when the mechanism was ready to have its factory tests.

A further minor controversy arose from an earlier proposal from the Astronomer Royal that the heavy weights which powered the clock and bells should be hung in the airshaft which was the central structural core of the clocktower and which had been provided for the ventilation of the House of Commons. This was referred by Phillips to Barry, who replied that he was unable to supply the information and that the matter should be referred to Dr Reid. At this time relations between Reid and Barry were very strained. Dr Reid, the ventilation engineer, objected strongly to the use of the airshaft, but after much discussion and many arguments it was agreed that a separate shaft be made within the tower, to accommodate the weights. This turned out to have been a very fortunate decision as, although Dr Reid had designed it to be a fresh air inlet shaft only, in which the weights and cables could have operated safely, it was found that the air system did not work. Dr Reid's scheme for introducing clean fresh air from the top of the clocktower instead of the polluted air from the lower levels was sound in theory, but the air-handling plant of his day was not capable of moving such quantities of air against the force of gravity. After Dr Reid's services had been dispensed with, a few years later, it was decided to reverse the air flow and to build a large induction furnace at the base of the tower airshaft, which would provide the suction to draw the air from the Debating Chamber of the House of Commons. This furnace, fired with coke, continued to burn, expelling the air, until the early part of the present century. How wise it turned out to be to have a separate shaft for the cables and weights.

Following the death of Louis Vulliamy in January 1854 and the collapse of Phillips' efforts to get the contract cancelled in July 1854, there was a period of quiet in the controversies whilst the mechanism, notwithstanding all difficulties, was completed in 1854, it was not possible to get the clock completed at this stage, as the clocktower, which had started eleven years earlier in 1843, had by then risen only to the height of the apex of the roof of the Commons Chamber. The final building drawings for the upper section of the tower and spire were not completed and signed until 1857. And, despite Denison's reminders, no action had been taken to design or order the bells.

Although the mechanism was highly successful on all the tests applied by the Astronomer Royal and Denison in the works, there was one matter of uncertainty, which there was now ample time to resolve. Perhaps Vulliamy was not altogether wrong in maintaining that no Great Clock with large and heavy hands subject to all winds and weather could meet the requirements for accuracy using the existing escapements. The escapement is the device by which the power of the weights is allowed to 'escape' to the hands under the control of the pendulum. None of the escapement designs in current use at that time was sensitive enough to meet the accuracy requirement, yet effective in preventing the effects of wind and rain on the heavy hands being reflected back on the pendulum and so affect the timekeeping. So Denison set out to invent an escapement which would meet the needs of the Great Clock. His success in this task was of such importance to the science and practice of horology that this form of escapement, commonly known as the 'Grimthorpe double three-legged gravity escapement', soon became virtually standard equipment not only for all turret clocks throughout the world but also for almost all pendulum clocks down to the present time. (It was of such importance to horology that more details are incorporated in a later chapter.)

It has been said that the hottest fires of controversy produce the purest metal of reason, and in this case there is no doubt that the result of this dispute was to produce the pure gold of an outstanding horological advance due to the application of the keenest scientific and practical minds to the solution of a problem which the Worshipful Company of Clockmakers had deemed insoluble.

Unfortunately this was the end only of the early disputes; there were many more to come, and there was a price to be paid for this first triumph. The deep ill will which had begun to build up between the clockmakers and the architect was to be the foundation of the disaster which was to strike more than 125 years later.

6   The Clocktower

'Let us build a city and a tower whose top may reach unto heaven.'
Genesis 11

Although the clocktower is the most dominant feature of the Palace of Westminster, this was never the intention of the architect. Barry had always intended that the Victoria Tower over the Royal Entrance to the House of Lords should be the most impressive feature. To this end he designed it to be the tallest and most massive square tower in the world in the nineteenth century.

In the early drawings the clocktower was shown as being much lower than it is today, but with the evolution of the design it became taller and somewhat slimmer. A factor in the greater height of the clocktower no doubt arose from the decision to build another tower in the centre of the building. This was never in the original façade but was provided as an afterthought to meet the demands of Dr Reid, the ventilating engineer, for a chimneystack in the centre to exhaust the air extracted from the Lords and Commons Chambers. The genius of Barry and Pugin transformed what might have been an ugly chimney into a masterpiece of grace and beauty, now known as the Central Tower, or by some St Stephen's Tower. For engineering reasons it had to be 300 feet high, and this had influence in taking the clocktower to 316 feet high. It is remarkable how many people think that the clocktower is higher than the Victoria Tower, which actually tops it by a small matter of seven feet.

It was with high hopes of the start of a great enterprise that on 28 September 1843 the first stone was laid by little Emily Kelsall, using a very beautiful silver trowel, exquisitely wrought and engraved, with an ivory handle, which now reposes with the Records of Parliament, high up in the Victoria Tower of the House of Lords. The inscription on the back of the trowel reads:

The
First Stone
of the
Clock Tower
of the
New Houses of Parliament
was laid by
EMILY
second daughter of
Henry Kelsall Esq.
of Rochdale
28 September 1843

———

Charles Barry Architect

———

Thomas Grissell
Samuel Morton Peto
Builders

The clocktower was not to be completed for more than sixteen years after the laying of the first stone, and Emily must have been grown up, and happy to have seen it finished at last.

The initial delays were due to many changes in the original design arising out of much parliamentary and national comment. Following the exhibition of the general views of the designs of the proposed palace in the Royal Academy in 1844, there were even comments in committee that a clocktower was not now necessary 'when almost every mechanic carries a watch in his pocket'.

About this time Charles Barry was urging the need for more accommodation in the Palace and advocating an extension of the plans by the erection of a three-storey Gothic-style building all round the perimeter of New Palace Yard. Had this been authorized, it would have abutted the west face of the tower. Indeed he went as far as to leave space for this addition on the lower part of the tower, and this can plainly be seen today. However, the Commons turned down the proposed extension with the result that the Palace was already too small when it was completed and has remained too small for Parliament ever since. Also in this period there were significant changes in the design of the tower, and Pugin, who was engaged on the detail drawings, advised Barry that twenty-three feet in diameter dials for the clockface would look better than the thirty-foot ones suggested earlier.

In 1852 there was an economy drive on public spending, and in an endeavour to reduce costs there was a change in the building contactor. This was perhaps unfortunate for Grissell and Peto, whose names had been inscribed with pride on Emily Kelsall's trowel and who were destined to build only the lower half of the clocktower. Their place was taken by John Jay, but the revised designs were slow to appear.

It seems surprising that at this early stage, when the main structural core and walls were started, and indeed carried up to half the final height, so little thought was given to the basic requirements for the clock and bells. In particular Barry had earlier specified a fourteen-ton great bell – as early as 1842, before the first stone of the clocktower had been laid. But the airshaft in the central core, up which the bell needed to be hoisted, was made only eleven feet by eight feet, in a tower with internal dimensions twenty-six feet square. Although no bell as large as fourteen-tons had ever been made in Britain, it required only a simple calculation from the proportions of normal bells to see that a fourteen-ton bell of orthodox shape would need a much larger shaft. By the time Denison was asked to design the bells in 1855, the height of the tower was nearly 150 feet, and it was far too late to change, so that the bell had to be designed to an unconventional shape, which could be hauled up the tower lying sideways in a cradle.

In the same way the structural walls around the airshaft conditioned the size and shape of the clockroom, which had again been determined without reference to the clockmaker. It might be thought that Barry had designed the accommodation with a view to using Vulliamy's clock, but this could not have been the case because the drawings supplied by Vulliamy required vastly more space than was necessary for

Dent's clock. It can only be assumed that the size was taken from the architect's previous experience in providing for small clocks on church towers. This complete lack of co-operation on the building requirements, for which the blame must be shared by all parties, necessitated re-design of the mechanism with the fundamental decision on the flyfans which was to bear such unhappy consequences over 125 years later.

The lack of co-operation also made for slow progress, and the final drawings for the belfry and the spire above were signed by Barry only on 24 March 1857. When Denison saw the drawings, he expressed grave doubts as to whether the structural ironwork was adequate for the weights and vibrations which would be set up by the bells. However, the strained relations prevented any deep reconsideration at that stage.

The basic construction of the clocktower is that of a self-supporting brick and stone structure mounted on a ten-foot-thick concrete raft, sunk down into the clay of the Thames basin. The external walls of brick faced with stone are three feet six inches thick, buttressed for the first eighty feet. The great loads of the tower spire, bells and clock are transmitted vertically down by the external walls and the massive brick core, housing the airshaft, to the concrete foundations. Structural ironwork is used on the lower stages only for the beams which support the fireproof floors. These are laid between the outer walls and the brick core, which gives added rigidity to the tower. The weight of the five bells in the belfry, aggregating twenty-one tons, necessitated a massive frame of riveted wrought-iron girders. The spire above the belfry is basically an iron structure with inclined cast-iron rafters with iron purlins and, like most of the original parts of the new palace, it is tiled with interlocking cast-iron roofplates. From the belfry floor there is a spiral iron staircase which winds up to the Ayrton Light. From there on, the only access to the high interior of the spire is by vertical iron ladders.

All the structural metal in the tower, as in the rest of the palace at the time, was of cast iron apart from areas of special stress which were of wrought iron. Every girder had to be 'linseeded' in the ironworks before delivery. This was done by raising it to a high temperature and then coating it with linseed oil to give it protection against corrosion. As it was not then possible to detect blowholes in the castings by visual examination, every girder was load tested, either by hydraulic jacks or more usually by placing a dead-weight load in the centre of the span, with the beam supported at each end, and then measuring the deflection. The beams which survived these tests were then further protected against rust by an extra coat of lithic paint before installation. This form of corrosion protection has proved remarkably good for well over a century.

The clocktower was built without external scaffolding so that, 'The tower seemed to grow . . . by some inherent vital power.' The internal frame, which rose with the tower, held a flat travelling crane, mounted on rails, which was used for lowering the external stone to the 'stonesetters' who built the walls, as well as raising all materials from ground level. It was powered by a 2½ horsepower steam-engine. The entire scaffold frame, which weighed sixteen tons, was raised by six manually operated screw jacks, which raised it three feet six inches at a time. This equipment was also used to raise all the structural ironwork for the belfry and the spire. It was found to be a most efficient and economical means of construction as the entire cost of this movable platform was only £700.

The interior of the clocktower has three shafts, all quite separate, and a number of rooms. One of the shafts on the south-east side contains a staircase which runs up to the belfry, passing the clockroom, with 336 stairs; the second is the weight shaft, within which the three weights of the clock move up and down on their pulleys, whilst the lower part of this shaft is filled with sandbags. For many years these sandbags served a dual role: they were there to cushion the fall of the weight or the pulley if a weight cable should fail, as indeed they have failed two or three times in the long history of the clock; also, for a long period they played a vital part in precautions against the flooding of the Palace, for which they were always available to be taken to seal the entrances through which water might have entered in the days before the building of the Thames Barrage. The third shaft was the old airshaft, by which Dr Reid had hoped to bring the purer air from the top of the tower down to the old House of Commons Chamber. This shaft is now disused, as the Chamber, as rebuilt after the bomb damage of 1941, has an efficient air-conditioning and purification system. A proposal was examined, to install a passenger lift in this shaft to make the clockroom more accessible to visitors, but the cost was found to be excessive.

From time to time stories have appeared in the Press about the clocktower leaning from the vertical. This first came to light in about 1965 when it was decided to excavate deeply into New Palace Yard to build a five-storey underground car-park. As this was to be close to the foot of the clocktower, it was decided that every possible precaution should be taken to ensure that nothing should disturb its foundations. To this end, before any work commenced on site, careful measurements were made to serve a datum line for the checks which would be made as the work progressed. It was found that the finial on the top of the clocktower spire showed that the tower was some nine inches out of the vertical.

The clocktower is 316 feet high with a base forty feet square, so that a deviation of nine inches at the top must be considered relatively small. Like the remainder of the Palace of Westminster, the tower is built on foundations sunk into the London Clay. It was feared that, with the deep hole so very close, there might be some movement of this clay which might affect the tower. To guard against any turning movement of the tower, it was decided to put an extra load of stone ballast in one of the rooms to compensate by exercising a contrary turning motion away from the direction of the excavation.

All the full and accurate measurements, which are still being made on an annual basis, show that the slight inclination of the top of the tower had not varied at all since the first measurements began some fifteen years ago. As no measurements were ever made before the present century, it cannot be established whether the inclination was due to initial settlement of the clay or to a minor constructional error at the time of the change of builder in 1852. The important thing is that the clocktower is safe and secure and, unlike the Leaning Tower of Pisa, is showing no sign of increasing its deviation from the vertical. It can be said therefore that the clocktower is likely to last at least as long as its predecessor, the tower of Great Tom, and with the present standards of loving care it may well endure much longer. The clocktower, like the Tower of Babel, has had many disputes, and there were doubts at times as to whether the contestants spoke the same language, but it did not prevent the completion of this most beautiful clocktower, with all its lavish ornamentation.

Finally much gilding was applied to the metalwork of the spire and the top finial, which consists of a ball and shower of stars. Under each face, in addition to the red and white shields with the crest of St George, there is the Latin inscription, in gold, which reads: 'DOMINE SALVAN FAC REGINAM NOSTRAM VICTORIAM PRIMUM' ('Oh Lord, Save Our Queen Victoria I'). This inscription is used very widely throughout the Palace of Westminster: it is carved into the stonework of the fireplaces, and into the woodwork above the lintels of the doors and windows; it appears emblazoned on the encaustic tiling which covers the flooring of the Royal Gallery of the House of Lords.

Prior to the current programme of cleaning the whole of the Palace, the last time the gilding of the clocktower ornamentation was renewed was in 1934, when some 26,000 sheets of gold leaf, weighing some 26 ounces of gold were used. It is remarkable how well this gilding had stood up to all the grime and acid corrosion of London in the middle years of this century. The introduction of smoke-abatement, and the fact that the boilerhouse of the palace no longer uses fuel with a high sulphur content, should also ensure that the newly cleaned and repaired stonework of the clocktower will remain in good condition for at least another century.

7 The Conflicts over the Bells I

Ring out ye crystal spheres
Once bless our human ears
Milton, *Paradise Lost*

The controversy over the design and construction of the clock mechanism was still rumbling on when it was displaced in the headlines by an even fiercer conflict over the bells. The original scheme, envisaged by Barry, was for there to be a great hour bell of about fourteen tons and eight quarter bells of various sizes. This idea was never drawn to the attention of the referees or translated into the contract requirements for the clock, which was designed, from the start, as a conventional mechanism suitable for working with a large hour bell and the usual four quarter bells. Indeed, for many years the provision of the bells as a separate contract was given little or no consideration. In 1852 Denison reminded the Office of Works that no bells had been ordered, and they wrote to the Astronomer Royal asking him if he would write a specification and act as referee for the design and construction of the bells. Professor Airy wisely declined this request on the very reasonable grounds that he knew nothing of the design and construction of bells.

Following this refusal in 1852, the matter was allowed to rest until, on the completion of the clock mechanism in 1854, Denison again wrote to the Office of Works, reminding them, once more, of the necessity of providing the bells. In February 1855 the Office wrote to Denison asking him if he would prepare the specification for the bells, again without any reference to the original idea of eight quarter bells. Perhaps it was as well that this idea had been forgotten as the mechanism was completed and accepted with the cams for the usual four bells only. Denison replied promptly with an outline manufacturing specification and was invited to act as referee for the construction, along with Sir Charles Wheatstone, a famous scientist and electrical engineer, and the Reverend W. Taylor, a well-known campanologist.

Denison was happy to accept these co-references, and all appeared well set to arrange the letting of a bell contract. Unfortunately Phillips of the Office of Works, without consulting him, added the name of Sir William Molesworth, the First Commissioner, to the list of referees. When Denison heard of this addition, he was furious and wrote immediately resigning his appointment, stating publicly that he would be no party to an arrangement of having a referee who knew nothing whatsoever about the subject! The Office accepted his resignation, losing the only one of the referees who knew anything about the design and construction of bells, and so the matter was again at a standstill.

Shortly afterwards Sir William Molesworth was given a more important appointment in the Government, and Sir Benjamin Hall was nominated First Commissioner in his place. Sir Benjamin could see that without Denison's knowledge and experience the project would remain at a standstill, so he restored the position on the appointment of referees and with great personal charm persuaded Denison to withdraw his resignation. The way was therefore clear for the issue of tenders.

There had never been a very large bell cast in England up to that time: the bellmaking industry had always operated on a rather local basis, possibly due to the difficulties of transporting large bells on the roads of the period. Some of the firms had long histories: Mears, the Whitechapel Bell Foundry, claimed that their firm went back to the year 1420 and that they were the only firm in the country capable of making such a large bell. Warners of Cripplegate were very keen to get the order and pointed out that they had just ordered two new furnaces for their foundry at Stockton-on-Tees. John Taylor of Loughborough was also a well-established firm with a good reputation for high-class bells. At that time there was a great demand for medium-sized bells for all the new churches going up to meet the needs of an increasing population. Today few churches are being built and of these not many have towers, and where these are built, it is quite usual for the sound of the bells to be reproduced electronically from a tape deck, so the number of bell foundries has declined everywhere, and today there are only some seven or eight known throughout the world. Fortunately the two that have survived in Britain are the Whitechapel Bell Foundry and John Taylor of Loughborough, both of which are historic and justly famed for their high standards.

When Denison was making his recommendations for tendering, he suggested that Warners of Cripplegate had the most efficient bell foundry but included that if competition was desirable then Mears, at the Whitechapel Bell Foundry, and Taylors of Loughborough (the firm had no connection with the Reverend W. Taylor, the referee) should also be allowed to quote. Unfortunately Mears, who like Vulliamy was at the top of his craft, refused to quote in competition with others, declaring that no other firm could make the bells. John Taylor put in the lowest tender, but this was not acceptable because they insisted on payment in advance. As the Government was not prepared to pay in advance for a bell which might not be satisfactory, the contract was placed with Warners of Cripplegate.

The bell was by far the biggest ever made in Britain up to that time, and it had that additional complication that it could not be made to the orthodox shape for a large bell as the architect had not allowed space in the airshaft to enable a conventional bell of this size to be hoisted up the tower. Warners, although happy to proceed with the four smaller bells were a little concerned about the size and shape of the great bell and asked if they could be supplied with a detailed design. Denison, that most gifted of amateurs, therefore produced a detailed drawing of the shape and thickness of a bell of the desired weight and dimensions to produce the required tone. He also specified that the consistency of the bell metal should be one of twenty-two parts of copper to seven parts of tin.

There was much argument at the time as to the correct mixture of metals which would give the best and most musical notes. It was about this time that a clergyman who wished his new church bell to have a silvery tone took all his family silver and fed it into the furnace where the bell metal was being mixed: alas, he was disappointed in the resulting tone. Today the latest scientific evidence gives the best possible constituency as seventy-seven parts of copper to twenty-three parts of tin, and all the best bells are made to this mix. This is approximately 23½ parts of copper to seven parts of tin, which suggests that Denison's mix was a little rich in tin, but working more than a century ago, it was not too far wrong.

It was agreed that, as Warners had recently installed two ten-ton furnaces in their Norton foundry at Stockton-on-Tees, they would be allowed to make the great bell there, provided they arrange the transportation down to Westminster. The four smaller bells were to be made at their Cripplegate foundry. The work of constructing the central core and the matching mould were put in hand in Stockton-on-Tees to conform as closely as possible with Denison's drawing.

After the heavy manual work in constructing this mould came all the anxiety on the day of casting. Even today, with all the appliances of science, the ability to produce an exact mix, and pyrometers to measure the exact temperature, the casting of a large bell is still a matter of some anxiety, as many weeks work and much money can be wasted by a single blowhole (the cavity in the casting where an air bubble leaves a void). How much more worry there must have been then, with the difficulties in getting the mix entirely right in both furnaces, and with no means of judging the temperature other than whether it 'looked right'. The pouring took one hour and was followed by 2½ hours of 'fusing'. Since molten metal occupies more space than solid, it is necessary to keep pushing the metal down to ensure that it fills all parts of the mould, and to bring all bubbles to the pour holes. This is done by repeatedly driving iron rods up and down manually through every pour hole until the metal has firmly set – hard work among the unhealthy fumes given off by the mixture of copper and tin.

When the sand mould was broken and the casting was seen to be intact, there were joyful celebrations with large quantities of beer consumed by the men who had striven so hard, under such difficult conditions, to make the greatest bell of its time. The jubilations spread to London, where there were widespread celebrations at the casting of the bell which was to sound over the capital.

The moving of so large a single load was a matter of prime concern in those days of poor roads, and it was too big to be transported by rail in the normal way. It was found possible, by clearing both tracks on a Sunday, to move the bell by rail the short distance to the port of West Hartlepool where it could be loaded on board a ship. A schooner, *The Wave*, was chosen to transport the bell to London since although she was a very small craft, she had the important ability of being able to unship her mast and so pass under London Bridge. There was, however, some difficulty in loading the great bell onto the ship. During the loading it became obvious that the bell weighed far more than the designed weight of fourteen tons. As it was being loaded onto the deck, the shear-legs gave way and the bell, which actually weighed sixteen tons, fell some eighteen inches onto the deck. Fortunately none of the men were hurt, but the damage to the ship resulted in *The Wave* being put into dry dock to have her deck straightened and a new foremast fitted.

In London there was much concern at the delays that had occurred, even after she had sailed from West Hartlepool, and there were strong rumours that the ship and her valuable cargo had been lost in a severe storm which had swept the North Sea. Fortunately *The Wave* had weathered the storm and on 21 October 1856 she docked safely at Maudsley's Wharf, bearing her precious cargo undamaged.

Amid scenes of public rejoicing by vast crowds of eager Londoners, the bell was transported from Maudsley's Wharf across Westminster Bridge on a heavy truck pulled by sixteen large white horses. The crowds of cheering people were so great that the police had much difficulty in controlling them and getting the bell through the gates into New Palace Yard.

As the clocktower was still incomplete, the bell was mounted on a temporary gallows at the foot of the tower. There it was struck by a six-hundredweight hammer for a quarter of an hour each week for ten months. The original intention had been to use a four-hundredweight hammer, but the size of the hammer had been increased because of the extra weight of the bell and because the skirt was found to be approximately one inch thicker than was shown on Denison's drawings. This increased thickness might have been due to inaccurate measurement of the mould, or it might have been the result of leaving the sand in the core too wet, so that it shrank with the heating from the molten metal. This greater thickness, which was extensive, would account for the extra two tons of weight which had had such serious consequences in loading onto the ship.

On 17 October 1857, almost a year after the bell arrived in London, the unbelievable happened: the tone of the bell went flat. A man was sent inside the bell with a candle and soon emerged to report that there was a major crack, four feet long, stretching upward from the sound bow. There were claims in the daily papers that light could be seen through the crack, but as the crack was only three inches deep and the thickness of the metal was amost 9½ inches in that area, this was probably a misunderstanding.

There was much bitter controversy as to whether the fault lay with Denison, for using too heavy a hammer (as was claimed by the manufacturers), or (as claimed by Denison) due to the manufacturers producing a poor casting. Full examination by Denison and the Reverend Mr Taylor showed that the crack was so extensive that it would be necessary to recast the bell.

Warners claimed that the bell had been delivered a year earlier and had been used regularly with a heavier hammer than they recommended, so they could not be held contractually responsible. As it was considered that a legal battle with Warners was not likely to be successful, the Office asked them for a price for recasting to a specification tighter than that which Denison had drawn up. When their price came in, it was considered unacceptably high, so it was decided to go out to tender for the recasting. On this occasion Mears of the Whitechapel bell foundry put aside the professional pride which had prevented his putting up a price for the previous competition, and was happy to put in a tender. In fact, he had been very sorry to have lost the opportunity of making the most famous bell in the world, for the prestige and sales value of such an order would have been tremendous, so he was delighted to have the chance of making a new bell from the broken metal of the old one. He put in a reasonable bid of £8.17s.4d. per hundredweight to recast it and, as this was the lowest price from a reputable firm, a contract was duly arranged.

On 17 February 1858 a large iron ball, weighing one ton 448 pounds was dropped on the bell repeatedly from a height of thirty feet, for a period of two days, until it was completely broken into fragments which could be loaded on carts. It was then found that, where the crack had started, there was a flaw in the metal, at the point where the two streams of molten metal from the two furnaces had met but had not fused together, leaving gas pockets not visible on the surface of the metal. Denison felt that he was vindicated and that the failure was due not to the use of the heavier hammer but probably to the coolness of the mould which had reduced the temperatures of the two streams of metal so that when they met they were too cool to fuse together and boil off the bubbles of gas. It was also probable that the temperature of the metal in the furnaces were too low for effective pouring, but at that time there was no means of measuring the temperature of molten metal.

At this time there was a popular jingle in London which ran:

> Poor Mr Warner is put in the corner,
> For making a bad Big Ben.
> Good Mr Mears, as it appears,
> Is to make us a new one – when?

Although the public were getting justly impatient at the many delays in getting the clock and bells which they had been promised some sixteen years before, it was not fair to put any blame on Mears. He lost no time in making the mould for the new bell and, profiting from earlier mistakes, was careful to ensure that the dimensions were precisely right by Denison's drawings. This time the core of the bell mould contained some 1,500 bricks and had been well dried out. This time Denison had stipulated that the mould must be heated for twenty-four hours prior to pouring to avoid the liquid metal from the various pour holes cooling before they fused together. It was the first time that such a technique had been employed in a British bell foundry.

The old bell metal, which was found to weight sixteen tons

930 pounds was melted down and purified in three large wood-fired furnaces before being poured into the preheated mould on 10 April 1858. This time, after the 'fusing' and 'rodding', which were done with more than the usual care and thoroughness, they were not in such a hurry to break the mould to see if the casting was good but waited patiently for it to cool off gradually.

The casting was inspected carefully by Denison and Taylor, who accepted that it was successful.

The bell has the royal coat of arms on one side and the portcullis of the Palace of Westminster on the other. Around the skirt is the following inscription, also cast onto the bell in letters of iron: 'The bell weighing 13 tons 10 cwts 3 qtrs 15 lbs was cast by George Mears, Whitechapel, for the clock of the Houses of Parliament under the direction of Edmund Beckett Denison in the 21st year of the reign of the reign of Queen Victoria and in the year of Our Lord 1858.'

The new bell was loaded onto a heavy truck, pulled once again by sixteen powerful horses, and proceeded along the Whitechapel Road, across London Bridge, along Borough Road and over Westminster Bridge to New Palace Yard. Crowds lined the route, but the police did not have quite the same difficulties they experienced with the earlier bell.

In New Palace Yard the clocktower, although now advancing rapidly, was not yet ready for the bells, so the new bell was mounted on the same gallows which had been used for the first bell. There it was sounded by the same six-hundredweight hammer. According to many reports, the note of the bell was in every way superior to that of the previous bell. (Nowadays bells are finely tuned by turning them on a lathe and removing metal until deemed correct by an electronic machine which measures the vibrations in cycles per second. Of course, no such machinery existed then, nor was it then possible to turn Big Ben on a lathe, so that the tone of the bell was entirely the result of good casting.)

By September 1858 the clocktower was sufficiently far advanced to be able to receive the bells, although the spire had still to be completed. The four quarter bells had been cast at Warner's Cripplegate foundry, with little difficulty except that one had been rejected by Denison and had to be recast.

The bells too were very large for quarter bells of their period, and indeed the largest of them was as big as the historic Great Tom of Westminster. (Details of the sizes and dimensions of these quarter bells are given in Appendix II.)

The raising of all these bells to the height of the belfry above the clockroom was a considerable task, not made any easier by the difficult relations between Barry on the one side and Denison and Dent on the other. There was some controversy as to whether the steam-engine which had been used to lift all the heavy girders for the spire, and indeed all the stone and brick used in the construction of the tower might be used to raise the bells. To the surprise of many, Barry totally rejected the use of steam for raising the bells on the grounds that it would cause too much vibration. This appeared very strange as the same little steam-engine which had been working so long in raising the stonework had caused no problems of vibration, and in any case the quiet turning of a steam-engine would cause vibrations which were microscopic compared with those which would occur when the bells were struck by their heavy hammers. Were the bitter conflicts and bad feelings between the architect and the clockmen the reason for this decision? Alternatively, it is possible that there was some anxiety because the construction of the spire above the belfry was not complete. In the long run it was decided that the raising of the bells should be put out to the structural ironwork contractor.

The raising of the quarter bells, using a large hand-driven 'crab' or winch of special construction, was not excessively difficult. The largest, weighing nearly four tons, took approximately six hours to rise the two-hundred-odd feet on 30 September 1858.

The lifting of the great bell was a major task as it was conditioned by the size of the airshaft. As previously mentioned, the raising of the bell had not been considered when the airshaft was built, and when Denison was asked to design the bell, the airshaft was already built to the height of 150 feet, with a space of only eleven feet by eight feet six inches. No fourteen-ton bell of conventional shape could pass up this duct so Denison compromised by designing the bell to be only seven feet six inches high and nine feet in diameter at the skirt. This he calculated could be turned on its side and, encased in a suitable cradle, drawn up the shaft, which would need to be lined with planking. (Plate IV)

The great bell was therefore turned on its side, and a wooden cradle was constructed around it. The cradle was fitted with friction rollers to guide it upwards along the planking lining the shaft. A strong chain had been specially manufactured, 1,500 feet long, with the metal of the links forged seven-eighths of an inch in diameter, with every link separately tested. This was coiled onto the heavy duty crab, which had been modified so that it could be manually operated by eight men working together. Commencing at 6 p.m. on 12 October 1858, the men started the lift, working in relays, and thirty-two hours later the bell was on the floor of the belfry 201 feet 3½ inches up. This was a laborious task, and many must have heaved a sigh of relief when it was safely secured.

Unfortunately this was not the happy ending for the Big Ben bell: there was still a long and hazardous journey to travel. At first all seemed well. After the bell had been placed in position in its collar, it was sounded not by the six-hundredweight hammer but from a light rope attached to the clapper suspended from the centre of the interior of the bell. In the normal way this clapper would never be used (and it has now been removed), and the bell would always be sounded by the hammer striking the exterior of the skirt, but, as with most bells, a clapper had been provided, and as the elaborate hammer mechanism was not yet in place, it was decided to try the note of the bell from its resting place in the tower. The rope attached to the clapper was pulled by Denison, down below, and this produced a very acceptable sound, which was appreciated by Londoners not only in New Palace Yard but throughout Westminster.

This happy beginning was, however, spoiled by the discovery that the collar through which the bell was suspended and indeed the whole ironwork of the frame supporting the bell were not strong enough. There had been earlier discord between Barry and Denison on the adequacy of the bell supports, and such further delays could not escape public recriminations. There was further controversy when the bell was fitted into its new collar, because it had been secured too tightly, affecting its clear ring. Denison was widely blamed for this in letters to the Press, although this easily corrected error was probably due to the over-enthusiastic efforts of some workman, who had been trained to fasten up every nut and bolt as tightly as possible. The matter was quickly adjusted, but Denison could be trusted to rise to any bait, and his letters of reply were truly vitriolic.

With the passage of the bells up the main airshaft, and their fastening to a secure structural framework and testing to general satisfaction, it became possible to start the installation of the clock mechanism in the room below the belfry. This, unfortunately, did not mean the end of the drama of the bells. The hottest parts of the controversies were yet to come. But at this stage the difficulties of the bell were interrupted by an acute controversy over the dials and the hands which had to go through all its stages before further testing of the bell could proceed.

8　The Completion of the Mechanism

'Vulgo enun dicitur: Iucundi acti labores.'
'Many have said: Completed labours are pleasant.'

Cicero

Although the clock mechanism was made in much its present form by 1854, there was no question of installing it, as the clocktower had only reached the height of about 150 feet at the time, and very much work had to be done before it achieved its final height of 316 feet. Furthermore it was necessary for the bells to be taken up the airshaft and duly installed before the mechanism was put in place. As Denison was not asked to undertake the design and specification of the bells until February 1854, it was obvious that there was more than ample time for full testing and the incorporation of any later ideas. The testing by the staff of the Royal Observatory, with frequent visits from the Astronomer Royal and Denison, was long and extremely thorough.

In April 1855, however, the Astronomer Royal expressed his approval of the standard of accuracy and general construction of the clock mechanism, and he wrote to the First Commissioner expressing his complete satisfaction with the mechanism and recommended that Dent should be paid the fair proportion of the final price. There then arose the problem of where to store the mechanism, which was overcome by Dent's agreeing to store the whole of the equipment in his works for the period required at no further charge. This was a most generous offer, considering the way he had been treated over the time when the Office was disputing the validity of his contract.

During the long years of this storage, Denison managed to

spare some time from his extensive legal duties, and his preoccupation with the design and detailing of the bells, on the consideration of means of improving the accuracy of the clock. Although the Astronomer Royal had been quite satisfied with the accuracy of the timekeeping, when the clock was fitted with Denison's first three-legged gravity escapement, he, Denison, was very conscious of the difference between the accuracy of the clock working under controlled conditions in Dent's works and the possible behaviour of the same mechanism when driving the massive hands under the worst conditions of icy winds and driven snow on the clocktower. To improve his movement further and to offset these external conditions, he continued experimenting with variations of the escapement he had invented for the clock. He tried a four-legged gravity escapement, which was fitted and worked very well for many months, but he was not fully satisfied even with this improvement. At last he came upon his ultimate, the double three-legged gravity escapement, which was finally fitted and which still functions on the clock today. Indeed, this escapement is still fitted to the vast majority of large pendulum clocks throughout the world.

Following the installation of the bells, it was possible to hoist the massive clock frame, with its huge winding-drums, up the airshaft and place it in position bridging over the weight shaft. Above this the heavy superstructure was erected to support the drive-rods geared out into four directions to propel the four sets of hands. It will, of course, be remembered that this was before mechanical gear hobbing was in use and so all the massive gear trains had to be cut laboriously by hand. These hand-cut teeth were far from uniform in shape and profile, so that each tooth had to be individually adjusted to mate in with its neighbours, with the gearwheels marked so that the mating of the wheels was always tailored so that they were engaged, tooth with like tooth in the same sequence. It was a tricky business before mechanical methods enabled tooth profiles to be standardized. The central roller bearings of the hands had also to be most accurately made as it would not be possible to repair these subsequently without the massive task of removing the hands.

The pendulum, which during all the trials had been

mounted on a bracket attached to the bedplate of the clock, whilst in Dent's workshop, had now to be accommodated in a cast-iron pendulum pit, sunk under the floor of the clock-room, with only the heavy suspension bracket, known as the pendulum cock, and its suspension spring, with about three feet of the pendulum rod, including the vital part which engaged with the escapement, visible in the clockroom.

Dent's men had to work hard and skilfully because there was much work to be done in the alignment of all the arbors, the running of all the wire ropes, some to stretch down to the pulleys from which the weights were suspended in the weight's pit, and some to operate the hammers through the bell crank levers. All this way done in very rapid time because their work was normally the last to be done before the clock could be started. The mechanism was complete and connections to the first two hands were made with difficulties which until then had been unforeseen.

9 The Conflict about the Hands

'Thus the whirligig of time brings in his revenges.'
Shakespeare, *Twelfth Night*

When the clocktower had progressed sufficiently to enable
the bells to be fitted and the mechanism to be installed, it was
possible to hope for the clock to be measuring time in the
fairly near future. But it was only then that the difficulties and
the problems of the hands began to unfold.

It had always been stipulated that the architect must be
responsible for providing the dials and the hands, as they
were an important part of the façade of the Palace. The only
stipulation made by Denison and the clockmakers was that
the weight of the hands, including the counterweights and
bosses, should not exceed two hundredweights. This was an
important provision as it governed the power which would
need to be available from the clock to move the four sets of
hands, aggregating eight hundredweights, plus all the weight
of the gearing and the long driving shafts.

A. W. Pugin undertook the detailed work of the dials and
made a design which is a joy to behold. The figures on the
dials are Roman numerals with the letters in unique form of
Pugin Gothic derived from those on the fourteenth-century
Studley Bowl, and these are incorporated in an elaborate
cast-iron Gothic tracery of exquisite design holding 312 pieces
of special opal glass in each face.

The only departure from the clockmaking tradition of
centuries past was that the four o'clock marking was shown as
IV and not the usual IIII. It is possible that Pugin did not
know of this tradition, and unfortunately relations between
the architects and clockmakers were never close enough for it
to have been communicated. This tradition may have been

based on an incident in the fifteenth-century when King Charles V of France was receiving the famous clock of Henry de Vick, which was to be installed in the Palais de Justice in Paris. The King objected to the figure IV on the dial and told the clockmaker that it should have been IIII. When de Vick dared to argue, saying that both forms were in common use in antiquity, King Charles said, 'I am never wrong. Take it away and correct it.' Since then the use of IIII on clocks has been universal. There is, of course, the possibility that dialmakers soon found that the use of IIII made for a better design balance with the figure VII on the corresponding place on the other side of the dial. The effect of these unusual characters on the dials of Big Ben has always been considered most elegant, but it does provoke a number of enquiries every year.

When completed, the figures and hands of Big Ben were painted a deep ultramarine blue, and the spandrels, (the spaces between the round of the dial and the square of the stonework) were a blue-green. With the red and white of the St George's crosses and the gold of the inscription, the clock faces must then have looked a very much more colourful sight than of recent years since the hands and the figures have been painted black. When the clocktower was cleaned in 1986 it was proposed that the metal work of the dials and hands should revert to the original blue colour. In view of the fact that blue was the colour of the Conservative Party, then in government, it was decided that it would be politically less controversial to continue to paint them black.

As Pugin died in September 1852, it is not clear who did the final detailing of the hands, but they were made to an elegant Gothic design in cast iron. Unfortunately each weighed over eight hundredweights and, of course, the mechanism could not hold them as they passed the vertical. Denison asked Barry to have them remade in hollow gunmetal, but when this was done and the new hands were fitted there were still difficulties. The minute hand was still too heavy so that it 'fell over' a minute or so under its own weight. This caused a further public controversy, with Barry writing to *The Times* that Denison had approved the design of the new hands. This would seem to have given Barry his revenge for all the arguments and acrimony of the past, but he had forgotten that

Denison was a pastmaster in such venomous interchanges. His reply to *The Times* covered so many of the issues concerning the history of the clock that it is reproduced in full, to show something of the bitterness occasioned by their many disputes.

Sir,
WESTMINSTER CLOCK

Our great architect's head has evidently been turned by his unusual run of luck. Hitherto he has been getting that pleasant little 'solatium' which architects do, on all his extravagancies and mis-carriages at Westminster, while other people have got the blame.

Architecture, ventilation, clock-making, dial making, bell-hanging, it is all the same. The building has cost three times the estimate, and is full of blunders and inconveniences, and for that Gothic architecture and Mr Scott are to bear the blame and suffer, and Sir Charles Barry's son, in the Italian line, is to get the benefit, if it can be managed, besides the building of the new Burlington-house without any competition.

The ventilation cost about a quarter of a million, and has to be finished by opening the windows in the vulgar way; and Dr Reid, whose ventilation of the old House, everybody says was perfect, is sent adrift and pronounced the impostor.

The clock is kept waiting for the tower for five years, and until Sir Charles and his friends were unwise enough to try to throw the blame publicly on me, everyone supposed it was all my fault.

The bell frame would not stand the striking of the bell, as I had warned his clerk of works it would not; but the sagacious Quarm takes care to tell his visitors how tight the bell was screwed up, and to suggest that as the reason why the frame shook; whereas it was screwed up tight by an architect's engineer, contrary to my intentions, and the frame was no better when it was made loose.

The dials and hands made by him cost £5,900, and the clock only £2,376, up to last April, and somehow or other it is managed to lump them together in a Parliamentary return, with £6,061 more of incidental expenses, neither of the clockmaker or the bell-founders, and the people exclaim, 'What a heap of money that clock has cost!'

So now, I suppose, he thinks he can persuade the public that Mr Fitzroy, who had all the facts before him from both sides, misled the House of Commons the other day, and that I am responsible for the hands made by Sir C. Barry being too heavy to go, and too weak to resist the wind.

I wish Mr Fitzroy had not contented himself with the facts, though he did so quite correctly, and had consented to the papers being printed. The shortest account I can give of the matter is, that Mr Dent gives credit to the Government for no less than 26 cwt. of old gun-metal, copper, lead, and cast iron, of which Sir C. Barry's minute hands and their counterpoises were compounded; and that the four new ones, which are a great deal stronger, weigh exactly 8 cwt., the very weight which I myself prescribed to him as the proper one, when I consented to his making them instead of Mr Dent in 1856.

To his statement that I approve those hands as ultimately made by him, and that I fixed them, or saw them before they were fixed, or had anything whatever to do with the fixing, I give the flattest contradiction within the compass of the English language. The fixing was as bad as the hands, and such as no clockmaker ever adopts, and such as rendered it impossible to make them balance in all positions.

As he had chosen to stir this question, I will now say that from the time I was first asked to take this business in hand until now, there has not been a single stage in it in which we have not been put to needless trouble, and the nation to needless expense by Sir Charles Barry's carelessness and blundering. The design of the clock had to be altered to suit his walls, the clockshaft was too wide one way and too narrow the other; the great bell could never have been got up at all if it had been made of the usual shape, though he himself fixed the weight, and therefore the size of it, in 1846; the clock was kept back for years because it has to stand over the only place where the bell could be got up by any contrivance; the clock room was too dark to work in; the staircase is now in the only dark corner of the tower, and has to be kept lighted with gas and has windows opening into the ventilating chimney, where charcoal is burnt while Parliament is sitting; and so I might go on with a number more of obstructions, moral and physical, which I have had the trouble of encountering and the satisfaction of defeating.

I am content with the success if Sir Charles Barry is with his percentage; at any rate, he shall have nothing else, he may depend upon it.

Yours obediently,
E. B. Denison

24th August 1859

In reading the above letter it should be remembered that in the mid nineteenth century it was quite the usual practice for even the best architects to receive commissions from sub-contractors for help in the design and installation of various components, and it would have appeared strange if commissions had not been involved in the designs for the casings of the many clocks of various types and sizes which Vulliamy had made for the Palace. It should also be remembered that Denison, alone of all those deeply involved, gave his time, skill and endless effort without any form of remuneration or expenses – even the work of Sir George Airy was part of his official duties as Astronomer Royal. Notwithstanding the many hard truths in this letter, it was quite unpardonable, between two such outstanding public figures, each at the head of a learned profession. It was quite understandable that, under these circumstances, the editor of *The Times* put an embargo on future letters.

When Barry's second set of hands was removed, it was found that heavy copper plates had been screwed to the back of the gunmetal hands and that the weight was actually heavier than the previously rejected cast-iron ones! It is probable that Barry had never seen these hands, or had them weighed, or he would surely never have rushed into the Press on the matter.

Denison now requested authority from the First Commissioner to take over the provision and installation of the hands and, when it was granted, designed and got Dent's to make new minute hands from hollow copper, made in the cross-sectional shape of two double Ds placed back to back. The width of this very light and strong construction was 9½ inches at the centre, running off to 5½ inches at the tips. Although they were fourteen feet long, the weight of these copper minute hands was only twenty-eight pounds, which with the gunmetal boss and the counterweight came to only two hundredweights. During a recent cleaning of the stonework of the clocktower, the opportunity was taken, whilst the scaffolding was in position, to remove and entirely inspect the hands, including radiographic investigation. To the surprise of many, these hands, which had worked for 125 years in all weathers, were in perfect condition. The only wear found was in the roller bearings, which, although not badly worn, were renewed because it might easily be another 125 years before they were examined again.

As the slower speed of travel of the hour hands made their extra weight less important, the gunmetal ones, made by Barry's sub-contractor, were retained and are still in good condition, with the heavy copper backing plates still in position. There were some minute hairline cracks on the gunmetal bosses, but these were not considered serious enough to merit any special attention, other than the tiny centre punch indentations which are normally enough to prevent such cracks spreading any further.

It was interesting that the opportunity to observe the movement of the hands from the scaffolding was sufficient to dispel a myth which had gained credence over the years. The clock has a 'two-second' pendulum which, through the escapement, allows the mechanism which drives the hands to give them a forward impulse every two seconds only. But the movement of the hands, as seen from the ground, appears to be continuous. This was always believed to be because the inertia of all the heavy masses of the shafts and hands, and the elasticity of the drives, smoothed out the irregularities of the two-second impulses so that the minute hand moved continuously. Close observation from the scaffolding outside, however, showed that the continuous movement was a visual impression based on the distance away of the eye and the persistence of vision. Seen from close quarters, the minute hand does not move in two-second jerks, nor does it move continuously, but it has a gentle surge forward and then a tiny swing back in a sort of harmonic progression which is very pleasant to observe. It is interesting to consider that the tip of each minute hand travels over a hundred miles a year in this rhythmical dance.

Following the starting of the clock, officially, on 30 May 1859, with only two dials having working hands, the remaining hands were quickly fitted and the clock was working apart from the sounding of the bells.

10   The Conflicts over the Bells II

Now see that noble and most sovereign reason,
Like sweet bells jangled, out of tune and harsh.
Shakespeare, *Hamlet*

The clock having started on 30 May 1859, Big Ben first struck
its hours in July. The quarter bells took a little longer to go
into service, but it was decided that they should start chiming
on 7 September, the day on which the public would be
celebrating the sailing of the new steamship *Great Eastern* on
her maiden voyage. The music of the chimes was greatly
appreciated in London, where this arrangement by Dr Jowett
and Dr Crotch from Handel's aria in the *Messiah*, which had
been played on the bells of St Mary's Parish Church in
Cambridge for some years, was quite new.

At last the 'King of Clocks' demanded by Viscount Canning had come into his own, and his voice resounded over the
roofs of Westminster and far beyond. But this happy state of
things was to last only a few short weeks before tragedy
occurred again. At the end of September 1859, whilst being
struck with the same six-hundredweight hammer, the great
bell cracked. In the *Daily Telegraph* of 3 October 1859
appeared a paragraph which read: 'The great bell of St
Stephen's tolled his last on Saturday afternoon, "Big Ben"
like his predecessor, is cracked and his doleful E Natural will
never again be heard booming over the metropolis.'

Fortunately this prediction was not to be fulfilled, but it
stirred up an even greater public controversy than all the
previous troubles. The long-suffering British public had been
very patient. After the laying of the first stone of the clocktower in 1843, they had hoped to see the completion of the
whole Palace in five or six years. Now, some sixteen years

later, they were again disappointed. The controversy in the Press swelled to unbelievable proportions, most of the articles and letters blaming Denison for a badly designed bell. Accused of specifying the wrong mix of metals and above all of using too heavy a hammer, Denison replied in his usual manner, pouring scorn on his ill-informed critics and claiming that the bell had been badly made.

A close examination of the surface of the bell showed a number of blowholes and flaws in the metal which had been skilfully concealed by filling them with a mixture of cement and bell dust. But Mears of the Whitechapel Bell Foundry was not prepared to accept Denison's statement that it had been badly made, and took out a libel action against him. Denison appealed to the Office of Works for permission to take samples of the bell metal for analysis, but the Office was not prepared to allow it. Relations between the Office and Denison became so strained that he was even refused entry to the clocktower. The libel action had to be settled out of court because the necessary evidence was lacking.

In the interim, arrangements were made for the hours to be struck on the largest of the quarter bells. It gave the note of B Natural in place of the E Natural of the Big Ben bell, but this system continued for nearly three years whilst the controversy raged.

At length the Office for Works agreed to allow Dr Percy, the famous analyst, to take samples from the bell, and he took one from the area near to the crack, and another from the top of the bell. These samples (which are now part of the Dr Percy Collection in the Science Museum) showed that the metal in the area of the crack was 19.4 parts of copper to seven parts of tin, whilst at the top of the bell the proportion was 22.3 parts of copper to seven parts of tin. These results showed a poor mix of the metal at the time of casting, as Denison's specification called for a uniform consistency of twenty-two parts of copper to seven of tin throughout. The low proportion of copper in the sound-bow area would unquestionably mean that the metal would be brittle just where it was struck by the heavy hammer. Denison was vindicated: it was the casting that was faulty due to a poor mix of the metals.

To Denison there was only one answer: the weakness in the composition demanded the breaking-up and recasting of the bell. The Office of Works, and indeed all those who had declared it to be a bad design, shrank from the magnitude of the task involved. To break up the bell it would be necessary to remove the mechanism entirely from the clockroom below as it bridged the airshaft down which the bell would need to be lowered. In addition there would be the necessity of dismantling all the carefully aligned drive shafts, the removal of the weights and pulleys, the relining of the airshaft with timber, and the cutting of the masonry walls to allow the bell to be got out of the tower. A further complication was that the clock, which was proving so useful to Parliament, would need to be out of action all the time it took to prepare the mould, make the casting good and true of a new bell, and then to have all the difficulties of getting it up the clocktower again. And for all this it seemed such a little crack. Instead of being over four feet long, as in Big Ben I, the crack was only some eleven inches long. (Plate XI)

The Astronomer Royal, Sir George Airy, was persuaded to give his advice on how best to cope with this unfortunate situation. For a pure scientist he came up with some very practical suggestions, as follows:

a) That the bell be turned a quarter to obtain a different striking surface.

b) That the weight of the hammer be reduced by approximately one half.

c) That a stout platform be provided under the bell, in order to safeguard the lower portion of the tower in the event of the bell's being broken.

These recommendations were accepted and the large hammer was removed and a new one weighing four hundredweights substituted. Fears of the consequences if the bell should fracture further were dispelled by building a stout platform below it; then the bell was turned, after a slot had been cut in the soundbow to stop the crack running any further. The bell, as turned, was found to have a good tone and has continued to be fully satisfactory in every way since then. Although the continual hammering has produced some flattening of the surface at the point of contact, it has never been necessary to turn the great bell again.

It will be recalled that Denison had always intended to use a four-hundredweight hammer on the great bell, but when he found that Big Ben I's bell was more than an inch thicker at the soundbow than was shown on his design, he deemed it necessary to use a heavier hammer to bring out the full sound of the bell. Why he did not return to the lighter hammer when Big Ben II bell was near to the specified dimension is not known. It might have been that he really thought that the heavier hammer produced a better note. At that time all such comparisons had to be made by the human ear alone and these were often very subjective. The original hammer has been kept and is exhibited, with the permission of the Serjeant at Arms, in the Centre Curtain Lobby of the House of Commons, adjacent to the Terrace, where it may be seen by visitors. It carries the following notice: 'This is the original hammer used for striking "Big Ben" in 1859. It was found to be too heavy, its weight being 6½ cwts. In 1862 it was replaced by the present one of 4 cwts.' With the fitting of the smaller hammer to the turned bell, the days of controversy came to and end.

11   Big Ben Triumphs

If you can meet with Triumph and Disaster,
And treat those two impostors just the same.
                              R. Kipling, 'If'

After the Great Bell had been turned and found to be
satisfactory and to have a pleasing note with the smaller
hammer, all was well with the entire clock, which was keeping
excellent time, as shown by the hands and the bells, and there
were no further troubles and difficulties for many years.

Big Ben had triumphed over all the traumas, the long years
of waiting, the bitter opposition, the frustrating delays, the
public controversies and the many disasters, big and small.
Before the Great Clock lay a century and more of very
peaceful industry and achievement during which it was to
become not only the symbol of Great Britain, but also the
most celebrated timepiece in the world.

Through much tribulation Big Ben had triumphed, and the
major credit for this great constructural and horological
achievement must justly go to Edmund Beckett Denison
(Lord Grimthorpe) who, for all his human failings, alone had
the genius, the courage and the tenacity to translate this
dream into reality. In 1860 he wrote:

So ends the history of the clock up to the present time, having
already seen the death of the three clockmakers, the architect and
the Commissioners of Works, whose names were involved in it.
What further vicissitudes it may have to go through, I cannot
pretend to guess, save as the future may be divined from the past.
Too many people have had to be disappointed, defeated and
exposed in getting there, for its existence to be easily forgiven, or
for any of its occasional failures, such as all machines are liable to,

not to be magnified into radical defects – if possible. Meanwhile anyone who has really accurate means of judging can observe that the huge cast iron machine, which has to drive through all weathers such a weight of hands as no other clock in the world, keeps better time than the best public clock you can find of the common construction and common size. And it should never be forgotten that the designer and supporters of the rival plan confessed that they could do no such things, and derided the possibility of making a clock of this size keep accurate time at all.

12   The Achievement of Accuracy

'Old Time, the clocksetter, the bald sexton Time.'
Shakespeare, *King John*

Before recorded history the measurement of time engaged the imagination of mankind, but the need for an accurate division of each day was slow to develop. The fundamental human need for food could safely be left to man's internal clock, which would remind him of the passage of time by the pangs of hunger, but such human clocks were soon found to be tremendously inaccurate in the measurement of time. So there were the few who found the need for a more accurate and systematic division of time. In climates blessed with abundant sunshine it was possible to gauge the passage of time by noting the position and length of shadows, but with the varying lengths of days this was complex. The first recorded clock known to history was the sun clock of Karnak of 1570 BC; with the advent of the sundial and later the water-clock, the division of time into hours became easier.

From the very earliest stages of history, those wishing for a more mathematical division of time have always operated on a duodecimal basis, i.e. with twelve as the key dimension. Why this was decided upon by man, who is a creature with five digits on each hand who is naturally oriented to thinking in tens, is lost in the mists of time, but the system has never changed; not even in this day when there is a fashion for decimal metrication. Perhaps it is because twelve is a much more versatile number than ten.

The early Babylonians, who were fascinated with numbers, decided long ago that twelve was the most effective basis for all measurements and used their symbol for twelve in the same way mathematically as we use ten. Their system of counting spread rapidly throughout the Middle East, where it was realized that it was essential for any government to have a numerical system, otherwise it could not levy taxes. This was never changed until Alexander the Great invaded Persia. His rather more simple Macedonians were accustomed to counting on their fingers and thumbs and could not understand the complexities of the Persian system. Alexander therefore decreed that ten should be the basis for calculations and measurement in the world that he had conquered. What a pity that the human race had not evolved with two thumbs on each hand, which would have given a more effective means of controlling tools and weapons, and might have influenced any such conqueror of the world to have standardized on a more versatile and effective system of calculations!

This standardization on the basis of ten did not however, affect the division of time, perhaps because Alexander was little concerned with clocks. The division of time into a twelve-hour day and a twelve-hour night had been accepted by the whole of the western civilized world of the period and nobody wished for a change. Even in the Far East, China had also adopted a twelve-based time system, but using periods of the duration of two of our hours. The ancient Chinese time system began at what we would call 4 a.m. and sequentially their Hour (two-hour periods) of the Cock, the Dog, the Boar, the Rat, the Ox, the Tiger, the Rabbit, the Dragon, the Snake, the Monkey, the Horse and the Sheep. This system has limited use by traditionalists to the present day.

The Japanese system up to the opening-up of the country in 1872 was also based on twelve, but in a manner which was entirely different and uniquely more complex than that in use anywhere else in the world. Under this ancient system the daylight period was divided into six equal 'hours' and the nighttime period also into six equal intervals. If such a system had been adopted in an equatorial country such as Singapore, where the daylight and the nighttime periods are of almost equal lengths and there is little annual variation, it would have been much simpler, but in the Japanese islands the length of the days and nights vary considerably. They do not vary quite as much as they do in Britain but, all the same, if the system was rigidly applied, the length of the 'hour' in daytime in summer would need to be almost twice as long as the night-time 'hour' at the same time of the year. In practice there were some adjustment in the official system by variations to the period of twilight, but the principle of the variations in the length of the 'hour' was accepted by all and rigorously applied, despite the fact that it did to some extent interfere with the natural rhythms of the body. It can be imagined that this made for very complex clocks, which needed to be adjusted, either manually or automatically, almost every day to allow for the variation in the different lengths of the daytime and nighttime 'hours'. Such a system did not permit of any degree of accuracy in time measurement and was likely to lead to much confusion. It was possible, and indeed widely used, only at a time when the economy of the country was relatively simple and remained isolated from other nations. The adoption of Western time-measuring systems must have been greeted with great relief by the majority of the population.

The division of the Western hour into sixty minutes and later the division of the minute into sixty seconds are also long established in the mists of time, and also represent the combination of the duodecimal twelve with the multiplier five, which gave these smaller divisions greater flexibility. Although these subdivisions are of great antiquity, it is interesting to note that it was not possible to measure a minute, with any accuracy, until the fifteenth century, and the second until the seventeenth century. It was not until the present century that it became really necessary to divide the second into very much smaller intervals, and here now we mix the measurements when we say that a computer has an access time of one nanosecond (one thousandth-millionth of a second).

The standards of accuracy of the early sundials and water-clocks were only barely up to indicating time to the nearest quarter of an hour, and there were requirements for greater accuracy which were partially met by the use of sandglasses and candle-clocks, although these suffered from the drawback that they were essentially short-duration devices, which relied upon human intervention to turn over the hourglass or to light a new candle. The desire to eliminate the inaccuracies caused by the need for human intervention led to the beginnings of the ancient art of horology. The invention of the mechanical clock was perhaps the first truly involved mechanism made by our early civilizations. The earliest compromise between a water-clock and a mechanical movement was the Su Sung clock made in China, which employed a large wheel fitted with buckets, which when filled tipped a balance and caused the wheel to move the regulated amount. It was intended that this should be of sufficient accuracy to be used to record early astronomical observations.

The first mechanical clocks in Europe came in the eleventh century and were mainly in the great religious houses and palaces where their chief purpose was to remind the occupants, by the sounding of bells, of the time for the various religious services and acts of devotion. In general most of the early ones had no hands or dials but gave their time by the sounding of the appropriate number of strokes on a bell. The early turret clocks were very primitive and were controlled by a 'verge-and-foliot' escapement. Most of them were what is known as 'blacksmith's quality', and their accuracy was such that they often gained or lost as much as half an hour a day. Indeed, they were often corrected by the use of a portable sundial!

When the astronomer Galileo, who invented the telescope, and first observed the moons of Jupiter, turned his mind to the possibilities of the pendulum, he could see its potentialities for the improvement of the accuracies of clocks; he was working on the development of a pendulum clock with his son when he died in 1642. Unfortunately his son also died before finishing a clock, and it was not until Christmas Day 1656 that Huygens completed the first pendulum clock. This led to the development of longcase 'grandfather' clocks in the eighteenth century and did much in inculcating the passage of time with a degree of accuracy upon the minds of the people. Turret clocks also began to show improvements in accuracy with the adoption of the pendulum, and standards of construction began to improve with the substitution of screwed or riveted frames in place of the earlier practice whereby frames were usually secured by wedges. Also a great many of the earlier clocks had their mechanisms altered to change the old horizontal swinging foliot for the vertical pendulum, and in some the 'verge' escapement was changed for an 'anchor' escapement.

THE CHRONOMETER

The next significant advancements in the science and engineering of horology came following the terrible naval disaster of 1707, when due to faulty navigation a fleet of four ships and over two thousand lives were lost on the Scilly Islands. In 1714 the Admiralty offered a prize of £20,000 (a tremendous fortune in those days – more than the equivalent of £1 million in modern currency) for 'Finding the Longitude'.

Although many diverse schemes were put forward, it was soon realized that the best hope of an accurate determination of position would come from a careful comparison between local sun time, when the sun reached its highest altitude at noon, and the time shown by a clock which kept the accurate time of London even when carried by a ship half way round the world. Of course, pendulum clocks were quite unsuitable for operating with accuracy under the rolling and pitching conditions experienced at sea, and a new type of clock had to be created.

Many and diverse designs were tried with little or no success until John Harrison entered the contest. He was originally a maker of wooden clocks but his first precision ship's clock was a massive brass affair with a balanced movement. He subsequently perfected his H4 watch which became the prototype of all future chronometers. It was an immediate success and was extensively used by the Royal Navy, including the voyages of discovery by Captain Cook. John Harrison did not, however, achieve his full reward until 1773, when he was eighty years of age, having, in addition to his contribution to horology, given to the Royal Navy and the British mercantile marine the advantage of being able to navigate with precision and so to make the country the greatest sea-faring nation of that period.

The precision given by these chronometers also led to Britain's becoming the cartographer of the oceans of the world, and as most of this work was done by survey ships of the Royal Navy, the Admiralty Charts are still the supreme authority. When Charles Darwin sailed on the historic voyage of HMS *Beagle* in 1831, he had to share his tiny cabin (so small that he had to pull out a drawer to make room for his feet when he went to bed) with no fewer than twenty-two marine chronometers, each packed in a bed of sawdust, on the shelves. The reason for this large number (including some made by Dent) was as much to compare the performances of the instruments of various makes as to establish with precision the longitudes of the capes, islands and rocks charted. It was one of Charles Darwin's prime duties to care for these chronometers and to record their performance. There must have been many occasions when he bitterly grudged the space they occupied when many of his prized specimens had to be abandoned for lack of room for storage.

The very high degree of precision craftsmanship necessary in the individual creation of each chronometer made these instruments very expensive until Edward John Dent introduced basic engineering principles into their manufacture, which made them less of the particular work of a very gifted craftsman and more the routine standardized work of a team of highly skilled engineering workers. This brought the price down so that more and more ships could be fitted. It also led to an improvement in standards of workmanship throughout the industry of providing domestic clocks, and to the development of many specialist devices, such as the chronoscope, which was a super accurate stop-clock. Another specialist device, for the use of astronomers was the sidereal clock which was designed not only to measure the time of the earth round the sun but also to allow for the movement of the sun through space. Thus a sidereal day is some 3 minutes 56.55 seconds shorter than a mean solar day. As can be imagined, the accuracy of the movement and the precision of its gearing to enable such a clock to be of value to even an amateur astronomer need to be outstanding.

THE INTRODUCTION OF STANDARD TIME

It may come as a surprise to many to learn that, even when such accuracy as the sidereal clock was possible, there was no standard time throughout the communities which dwelt upon the small islands of Great Britain. Even when Big Ben was completed, it was designed to be accurate by 'London Time'. Most of the towns and villages outside London set their public clocks by sundial and, of course, there were quite large variations in the times between those in the east and those in the west. This first became noticeable on the stage-coaches which were supposed to run to time, but then it was of little importance.

It was the coming of the railways in the 1840s which brought out the need for greater accuracy and uniformity. As nearly all the railways converged on London, they were anxious to run their trains to London Time as their standard. This was of little importance to lines running to the north, but the Great Western Railway had much trouble on all their lines to the West Country, where the time at Bristol was some ten minutes behind that of London. A Bill was placed before Parliament in 1848 seeking to standardize the times but, in the face of strong opposition due to local patriotism in the shires, it was thrown out. This led to the standardization of what came to be known as 'Railway Time', which was more acceptable diplomatically than London Time, but it was not always recognized by some local councils, who continued to set their public clocks by sundial. Indeed at this period, some clocks, including that of 'Great Tom' at Oxford, had an extra hand which showed Railway Time.

It was not until 1880 that the 'Definition of Time Act' was passed which standardized all time in the British Isles on Greenwich Mean Time. This somewhat belated Parliamentary standardization, coming twenty-one years after Big Ben had started to set the time for London, recognized what had already been accepted by seamen of all nations as the navigational standard time for chronometers throughout the world. Sir George Airy, the Astronomer Royal, had instituted the Time Ball at Greenwich, and when this dropped at 1 p.m., all the shipping at the Port of London (then by far the greatest port in the world) set their chronometers by it. It was usual for ships at sea to check their chronometers against those of any ship which had recently sailed from London.

In the United States of America the problems of east to west time were far greater than in Britain, and when it was necessary to fix time zones across that continent they needed an established meridian as a basis. Naturally they chose Greenwich, which was the generally accepted navigational meridian for all seamen.

In October 1884 the nations of the world gathered in Washington to frame a treaty for the establishment of a Prime Meridian for the world. In a surprisingly short time, on 13

October 1884, it was passed that Greenwich should be that meridian, with only one country, San Domingo, opposing, and only two countries, France and Brazil, abstaining. Thus Greenwich Mean time became the basic standard time for the whole of the globe. Since then its use has been further extended, as it is used as the basis of time for all extra-terrestrial voyages in the solar system.

It will be appreciated that the standardization of time systems was a pre-requisite for the effective use of the possibilities for the accurate and universal time measurement which had been made possible by the advances in horology.

THE ACCURACY OF BIG BEN

Although the introduction of the chronometer had its effects on the general improvement on the accuracy of domestic clocks, it had virtually no influence at all on the building of turret clocks for at least fifty years, as it was felt that the problems of this type of clock were completely different. The great contribution of the design and construction of the Great Clock of Westminster to the science and practice of horology was that for the very first time it showed that it was possible for a large clock (and for many years Big Ben was by far the largest in the world) to have a standard of accuracy previously unknown.

The initial criterion of accuracy for the Great Clock laid down by the Astronomer Royal was that it should strike the hours with an accuracy of one second. This may not be considered a very high standard in the present age of quartz crystal controlled watches and clocks. But 140 years ago it was deemed by the Worshipful Company of Clockmakers so impossibly high for a turret clock that they addressed a memorandum to Parliament stating their considered professional opinion that the Astronomer Royal's demands were impossible. Indeed, it was only by Dent's gifted application of Denison's inventive genius that this seemingly impossible task was accomplished.

The accuracy of a conventional pendulum clock depends on meticulous workmanship throughout, but in addition there are two locations where the greatest precision is most important. The first of these is the pendulum and its 'cock' (the clockmakers' term for the suspension bracket). It is vital that the pendulum cock be firmly anchored to a rigid foundation completely free from vibration. Denison achieved this by having a massive cast-iron pendulum cock built into the thick structural wall which went down to the foundations of the clocktower and rested firmly on the ten-foot-thick concrete slab. The cock was thus completely independent of the clock frame and free from any vibrations caused by the mechanism or the bells. The pendulum was suspended from the cock by the pendulum spring, a piece of high-grade spring steel three inches wide and one sixty-fourth of an inch thick, with a free length of five inches. This suspension spring allowed the pendulum to swing freely, with the only contact between the pendulum rod and the mechanism being through the gentle, intermittent movement of the escapement.

To achieve accuracy the pendulum must be safeguarded against the effects of changes in temperature and movement or changes in density of the surrounding air. To guard against the effects of temperature changes, Denison compensated the pendulum by making the rod of zinc enclosed in an iron tube so that the expansion and contraction of the zinc should counter the similar temperature effect on the iron and enable the total length to remain constant under varying temperatures. To allow variations of temperature to reach both metals simultaneously, the iron tube is slotted. To minimize the effects of air movement, the pendulum has the greater part of its length enclosed in the cast-iron pendulum pit, which is a box about ten feet high by four feet wide by three feet thick sunk into the clockroom floor. As the pendulum is what is known as a 'two-second pendulum', it is thirteen feet long to the centre of gravity of the bob and takes four seconds to do a full cycle and has a total weight of 685 pounds. There are no means of guarding against variations of the density of the air so that alterations of barometric pressure can be recorded and compensated for only by human intervention in the manner to be detailed later.

The second important location for the preservation of the accuracy of the movement is in the design of the 'escapement', the mechanical device which allows the power of the weights to escape to the hands at a rate determined by the pendulum. When the Great Clock was first considered, the only two principal forms of escapement deemed suitable for large turret clocks were the dead-beat Graham style and the dead-beat Lepaute style pinwheel escapements. Denison tried these and at least six different types of escapement on the clock mechanism at Dent's factory between 1854 and 1859 whilst awaiting completion of the clocktower. In addition to the dead-beat escapements there was in existence the simple Bloxam gravity escapement which has always been considered too delicate to handle the very heavy stresses of a turret clock.

After much experiment with unusual forms of dead-beat using a three-legged escape wheel, Denison evolved a combination of the three-legged wheel, which he had previously tried to use to improve the dead-beat escapement, to a form of the gravity escapement, with the three pins arranged to lift and lock two gravity arms, instead of impulsing the pendulum directly. This had the unique merit of the detachment of the pendulum from the train of gears so that the wind and weather stresses and strains on the hands could not be reflected back to affect the smooth motion of the pendulum. This was the horologist's dream come true – the true gravity escapement was evolved. It was not, however, accepted at first, and the Astronomer Royal would not hear of its being used on the Great Clock, as he said that he had proved mathematically that it was a failure! However, following much pressure from Denison and Dent, he did agree to this escapement's being tried out on a clock at Greenwich, where it was a notable success. These practical tests convinced the Astronomer Royal, and he wrote to Denison: 'I have tried your escapement in the most malicious way, and shall endeavour to get it into Westminster.' At that stage in their relationship, however, the Astronomer Royal's approval would have been something of a formality as Denison was acting very much on his own; all the same he was no doubt pleased to have this endorsement.

This did not stop Denison taking his designs further, and he passed on to the 'four-legged gravity escapement' which he tried on the clock with some success; then he constructed the 'double three-legged gravity escapement', which had the advantage over its predecessors that it reduced the pressure on the 'stops' or locking pads on the gravity arms still further. Indeed, the pendulum is kept swinging by a couple of only one ounce falling one inch at each beat of the pendulum. This was the greatest horological advance in turret-clock design for many centuries and has since been adopted for most pendulum clocks, including those of the 'grandfather' type.

That neither Denison nor Dent made any move to take out patents for this great innovation is not at all surprising, since Denison never showed any desire to make money out of the endless work he put in to perfect the Great Clock, but it is noteworthy that in Dent's book *Clock and Watch Work* he comments, 'As it is not patented, it may be made by anybody.' Notwithstanding this freedom to manufacture without fee or acknowledgement, it is perhaps a tribute to Denison's fine contribution to horology that a very large number of clocks by other makers, including the great clock of St Paul's Cathedral, are stamped 'Grimthorpe's double three-legged gravity escapement' (Denison had been raised to the peerage as Lord Grimthorpe).

Strangely enough, this new escapement, which was specifically designed for use on Big Ben, was first employed on another clock under even more trying environmental conditions. This was because the Big Ben mechanism was still awaiting the completion of the clocktower. In the interim Dent and Denison made a clock for Fredericton Cathedral in New Brunswick, Canada, where the winter temperatures could be as low as forty degrees below freezing, and the hands, although much smaller than those of Big Ben, were very subject to ice, snow and high winds from whose effects the escapement was successful in isolating the pendulum. A diagram of the escapement is given in Fig. 3, and the dimensions are given in Appendix II.

In the Astronomer Royal's original conditions, he called for a special telegraph line from the Greenwich Observatory so that the accuracy of the Great Clock could be monitored against Greenwich Mean Time. In 1863 this link was installed and the exact time was compared, ever hour, with the time shown on the clock. For this purpose electric signals were taken from contacts which are still in existence behind the bronze twenty-four-hour dial on the clock mechanism. This arrangement, which operated with very satisfactory results for seventy-seven years, was discontinued in 1940, when the special telegraph line was destroyed by enemy action. It was

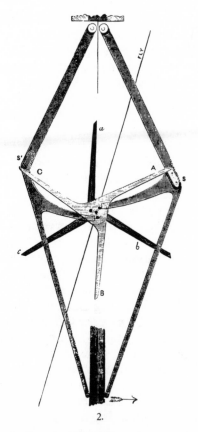

2.

3   Double Three-Legged Escapement

then felt that the accuracy of the Great Clock had been amply demonstrated and that it was not worth the expense of the renewal of the ground line. The latest report which covered the period of 290 days up to June 1939 showed the accuracy to be as detailed below:

Error	Number of Days
Not greater than 0.2 sec.	93
Not greater than 0.2–0.5 sec.	95
Not greater than 0.5–1 sec.	86
Greater than 1 sec.	16

At the present time the accuracy of the clock is checked three times a week, when it is being wound, and a log and a graph of its accuracy are kept, together with readings of temperature and atmospheric pressure. There are no longer direct checks from Greenwich but the time is checked from the telephone TIM by stopwatch.

The methods of measuring time have varied since Sir George Airy was Astronomer Royal, and Greenwich Mean Time has become the acknowledged standard for the world. It is checked constantly from observations and adjusted for internationally agreed values for the annual fluctuations of the spin of the Earth and polar variations. This is applied to time observations in the derivation of the uniform time system known as UT2, using ring crystal clocks, which are constantly compared with the atomic clock or caesium resonator at the National Physical Laboratory which is stable in its frequency of 9,192,631,830 cycles per second, and with other international time standards. The Greenwich Time Signal is transmitted by dots in the form of pulses on a thousand-cycles-per-second tone. The Post Office have their own ring crystal clock which is constantly compared with Greenwich, and the TIM signal is given by recorded time messages from a human voice, interspersed with dots similar to those of the Greenwich Time Signal. It is understood, however, that in the near future TIM is to be completely computerized. At the present time the accuracy of Big Ben remains within the range set by Sir George Airy in 1846, with very little difficulty, and this has proved fully satisfactory to the BBC for world broadcasting, but if Big Ben was ever as much as two seconds out, it would lead to very strong complaints.

PENNIES ON THE PENDULUM

One type of inaccuracy, against which it was not possible to guard at the time the clock was made, was due to variations of barometric pressure in the atmosphere. These fluctuations cause small variations in the air friction on the pendulum, and the only way of minimizing this would have been to run the pendulum in a completely sealed enclosure, or preferably in a vacuum, which would have been quite impracticable at the time. Instead a very simple method of correcting such small errors was devised long ago. This consisted of adding or removing pennies from the boss of the pendulum. With the weight of the pendulum at 685 pounds, the addition of one old-style penny, weighing one ounce, caused the clock to gain about four-tenths of a second in twenty-four hours under stable atmospheric conditions. (Plate X)

Questions are sometimes asked as to why, since Britain changed to decimal coinage, new pennies are not now used. In fact, any small weights could be used, but there were certain advantages in using the old coins as the exact weights of old pennies and halfpennies were known, and their use had been well tried for more than a century. Furthermore, there was never any need for extra coins, as those added on one day would probably need to be removed in the next week or so. To mark the major reconstruction of the chimes in time for the Loyal Addresses from Parliament to Her Majesty the Queen on 4 May 1977 for Her Silver Jubilee, one of the special silver Crown pieces minted for the occasion, with a suitable inscription, was substituted for other coins on the pendulum.

THE ACCURACY OF STRIKING

The fundamental requirement in the Astronomer Royal's specification of 1846 was for an accuracy to one second on the striking of the hour, and to this end the striking mechanism needed to be as precise as the timekeeping. Here Denison encountered difficulties as the old remontoire system, working from a normal cam rotating once every hour, was not nearly accurate enough, and with the two-second advances of the gear train under the gravity escapement it was necessary to devise a very definite and robust method of discharging the let-off lever. An ingenious mechanism incorporating a 'precision let-off' was devised by Denison whereby a snail (cam) on the fifteen-minute wheel acts early to release the locking arm in what is heard in the clockroom as the 'warning click', some two seconds before the hour strikes. Then, half a second before the hour, it allows the locking arm to rotate completely with considerable force, to overcome the friction of the system; the striking barrel is thus released, under the speed control of the flyfan, to turn the striking wheel. This has ten massive cams of involute profile, faced with steel tips 2½ inches wide, which engage the heavy lever which partially raises the already lifted hammer and releases it, suddenly, at the precise second the dial on the mechanism moves to sixty, and so strikes the hour.

It will be remembered that it is the first stroke of the Big Ben hour bell which gives the exact time, unlike the Greenwich Time Signal, transmitted on the BBC, where it is the sixth pip which gives the time. For those interested in extreme accuracy, it is well to remember that, due to the relatively slow speed of sound, it is necessary to add one second to the time for every three hundred yards the listener is away from the clock, when hearing directly. This does not, of course, apply when hearing it on the radio as the electro-magnetic waves travel at the speed of light.

The chimes which sound the quarters are not accurate measurers of time, although Denison claimed they could be set within two seconds. However, the fourth quarter must be set to start chiming a full twenty seconds before the hour in order to let the sound of the quarter bells die away before the hour bell is struck, clearly and distinctly, exactly on time. The lack of exact precision of the quarter bells does not prevent their being used extensively by the BBC, especially on the World Service, as they deem them quite accurate enough for normal broadcasting purposes.

13 Big Ben in Wartime

A time to love, and a time to hate; a time of war,
and a time of peace.
Ecclesiastes

The years that followed the completion of the Great Clock were essentially ones of peace and prosperity for Great Britain, at least as far as London was concerned. True there were wars in the Crimea and South Africa in which the country was involved, but distances were far and communications so difficult that the effects were small. London was, however, greatly affected by the major wars of the twentieth century, but through all the scenes of death and destruction the hands of Big Ben continued working with the customary reliability and accuracy.

When the Zeppelin raids started in the First World War and London was the major target, the bells of Big Ben were silenced so that their sounds would not betray the location of Parliament to these quiet, low-flying airships. The comforting and reassuring music of the bells was greatly missed by many of the residents of Westminster – especially the children. The sound of the bells was restored for the striking of the eleventh hour of the eleventh day of the eleventh month 1918 to mark the end of hostilities, when the people of London came flooding out onto the streets at the clamour of the bells – which, in those days before broadcasting began, was the first joyous news that the war with all its grief and horror was at an end.

In the Second World War it was not considered necessary to silence the clock bells, as aircraft were flying so high and were so noisy that sound location was not important. So, though the lights were out, the pleasing notes of the bells continued at a time when the ringing of church bells was prohibited, as they were to be used only as an invasion warning. However, before war was declared, the lights on the clockfaces and the Ayrton Light were extinguished, on 1 September 1939, as a precaution, and they were only to be lit again in a little ceremony by the Speaker (Colonel Rt. Hon. D. Clifton-Brown) at 10.15 a.m. on 30 April 1945, after the conclusion of the war in Europe.

Big Ben was destined to play a larger part in the survival of the free world than was envisaged when the lights were extinguished in September 1939. In response to the requests of many noted churchmen and other leaders in the country, the 'Big Ben Minute' was inaugurated on Armistice Sunday, 10 November 1940, at a time when only Britain, battered but unbowed, stood against the conqueror of Europe. The Big Ben Minute was started by the substitution of the chimes and the nine strokes of Big Ben for the nine o'clock time signal on the radio every day. All the freedom-loving peoples of the world were urged to keep silent for one minute, during the sounding of the bells, for reflection on the high ideals of Freedom, Justice and Unity, to build a better and fairer world. Everyone was urged to think, during this minute, of the men in the Armed Forces and others from whom they were parted by the war, especially their nearest and dearest.

This appeal had the greatest possible effect, and millions of people throughout the world, including a multitude in occupied Europe, made a practice of observing this silent Big Ben Minute, whether they could hear the bells on the radio or not, and reflecting on husbands, wives and friends separated, and on their ideals and aspirations for the future. The joy and fulfilment experienced by so many led to calls from all over the world for Big Ben to be broadcast more often so that those for whom the nine o'clock time was unsuitable, due to time differences, could still feel the comradeship of the bells at other times. This was agreed, and on the Overseas Programmes the chimes of Big Ben were played up to forty times a day. Americans used to call it 'the Signature Tune of the British Empire'. It has been claimed that the thoughts aroused by the music of the bells did much to raise morale and keep alive the courage of many people whose lives were devastated by the ravages of war. Following the end of the war, many kept up this practice of a silent minute, for many years, to think of their memories and of their hopes and thankfulness.

The Houses of Parliament were damaged by air raids on fourteen occasions during the 1939–45 War but Big Ben continued to operate as accurately and reliably as ever. Even in the great raid of the night of 10/11 May 1941, when the flames from the burning Commons Chamber, immediately below, mounted as high as the clockroom itself, the clock continued working, the hands showed the correct time and the bells thundered out their message among the blasts of the bombs and the crashing of the anti-aircraft guns. Some of those fighting the fires below thought the message one of defiance, others thought it one of hope. The sounds of the battle were picked up by the microphones, as the hours struck, and were carried to far-off lands with the music of the bells. Many prayed that London and Big Ben might be spared the utter devastation of destruction, and many listened again the following day, hoping to hear those greatly loved tones once more, and with joy heard that the great heart of London was as strong as ever.

The records of the Luftwaffe, found after the end of the war, showed that this was not a planned, deliberate attack on the Palace of Westminster, but in it three people died and the Commons Chamber was utterly destroyed. One large bomb went through the roof of the magnificent Chamber of the House of Lords, destroying all the beautiful stained glass in the windows, but most fortunately it did not explode, and the bomb disposal units did heroic work in removing it without further damage.

On the same night the clocktower was struck by what was either a small bomb or a misdirected anti-aircraft shell – which, has never been fully established. This did some damage to the stonework of the belfry and the ironwork of the steeple above, whilst the glass of the south dial was shattered. Big Ben treated such minor damage with lordly disdain and continued working as if nothing had happened, and with an accuracy of within 1¼ seconds of GMT. The pride of the Great Clock was, however, humbled later that year when a carpenter carelessly put down his hammer on the edge of the mechanism and it fell in and stopped the clock. How ironical that this negligent act should have accomplished the stoppage of the great mechanism which had stood up to the night of fire and fury! There were suggestions 3½ years later, when the suspension spring of the pendulum fractured, that it might have been weakened by the shock of the explosion. It was, however, also contended at a meeting of the Institution of Mechanical Engineers in 1981 that the suspension spring had been under-designed and that a thicker spring should have been used. This was not accepted by the former Resident Engineer, who pointed out that in 130 years of service only one suspension spring had failed. He calculated that before failure the spring had flexed over a billion times and suggested that for any mechanical system to have served eighty-five years of continual heavy duty twenty-four hours a day was the sign of a very accurate design. This seems to be borne out by the fact that the replace spring, of identical design, has already flexed half a billion times in forty-five years with no difficulty.

The broadcasting of the bells had caused some little alarm in remote localities due to the microphones picking up the sounds of the air raid sirens, which had on occasion been mistaken for those of the local siren. This came to a head during the worst period of the flying-bomb attacks in 1944, when it was feared that the sound of explosions, picked up by the bell microphones, might assist the enemy in the calibration of these missiles. Up to this date the sound of Big Ben had always been played 'live' directly from the microphones in the clocktower; in view of the serious security problem posed by the assistance these extraneous sounds might give, it was decided to suspend the 'live' transmissions on 16 June 1944. Instead recordings of the chimes and strikings were played from a soundproof cellar under Broadcasting House. Great care was taken to synchronize the recordings exactly with Big Ben to give the usual accuracy of the time. Notwithstanding all the assurances given at the time, there were many who feared that Big Ben had really been damaged by enemy action, and there was much relief when direct 'live' transmissions were resumed on 8 September 1944, when it was established that the flying-bomb sites which had been attacking London had been overrun.

On 8 May 1945 Big Ben again heralded the end of a great

conflict. After the great bell had struck 3 p.m., Winston Churchill announced that the war in Europe had been won. That night Big Ben was floodlit, and after the clock had struck nine o'clock His Majesty King George VI delivered a message to the world.

Big Ben also struck the hour of total victory at midnight on 14 August 1945, when Clement Attlee, the new Prime Minister, announced quietly that the war was finally over.

14 Big Ben: Superstar

> Ring out, wild bells, to the wild sky,
>   The flying cloud, the frosty light:
>   The year is dying in the night;
> Ring out, wild bells, and let him die.
>
> Ring out the old, ring in the new,
>   Ring happy bells, across the snow,
>   The year is going, let him go;
> Ring out the false, ring in the true.

When Tennyson wrote these lines for 'In Memoriam', he was probably thinking of the similar chimes of bells, although on a smaller scale, from Great St Mary's Church, when he was at Cambridge, but there can be little doubt that these lines were in the mind of the Programme Director of the British Broadcasting Company (as it was then called) when he was inspired to arrange a special surprise for listeners at the end of the year of 1923. A temporary line had been rigged along the Victoria Embankment from a microphone placed on the roof of No. 1 Bridge Street, opposite Big Ben, and run to their then control room in Savoy Place (now the Institution of Electrical Engineers). And to the great surprise of all those listening the last moments of the Old Year were rung out to the joyous chimes of the quarter bells, to be followed by the slow, majestic strokes of the Big Ben bell to welcome in the New Year.

Even though the reception on the crude crystal or valve sets of those days must have been poor, the public response was tremendous, and to meet the insistent demands from one and all, the first regular broadcasts of the sound of the bells to give 'Big Ben Time' to Britain were started on 17 February 1924.

They have continued ever since, to make Big Ben the most frequent broadcaster ever known and the Radio Superstar of all time.

More than fifty years earlier Edmund Beckett Denison, then Lord Grimthorpe, had expressed the wish 'that there could be some means of sending a time signal, at regular intervals, to every town and village in the land'. How remarkable that the Great Clock of Westminster, for which he had fought so valiantly and which had been achieved so splendidly, should be the instrument by which this long-held wish should at last be realized.

When the BBC celebrated its sixtieth birthday with a grand service in St Paul's Cathedral, on 12 July 1982, it was appropriate that the tones of Big Ben should feature prominently in the 'Medley of Broadcasting Sounds' played, as part of the service, under the Great Dome. The music of the bells had been regularly broadcast for more than fifty-eight of the sixty years being celebrated. At this service George Howard, Chairman of the BBC, stated that the World Service, which uses the chimes and striking of Big Ben more than a dozen times each day, is heard by more than 150 million people every week, scattered all over the globe.

The microphone on the roof of No. 1 Bridge Street had served its purpose well on New Year's Eve 1923, but tests had shown that the traffic noises were too strong, on a normal day, to permit regular transmissions of an acceptable quality. The sound of the bells had always been heard and loved as it resounded in the area adjacent to the foot of the tower, where the metallic sound had been somewhat attenuated and softened by the reflections and refractions of the stonework. The positioning of the rather rudimentary carbon microphones of that era was therefore considered critical.

Following various tests in the belfry it was decided to try the use of a microphone inside a football bladder, and to locate it on the gallery above the gantries from which the bells are suspended. This proved effective, and the sounds broadcast were acceptable to the listening public, so this very unorthodox system of a microphone within a bladder continued for some six years until improved microphones became available in 1930. Duplicate STC microphones of a similar type are still in use in the same location today. A remotely controlled amplifier was installed in a small cubbyhole off the staircase, at the foot of the tower, connected directly with Broadcasting House when it was opened. Duplicate amplifiers are installed in the same place today, connected by land line to Bush House, Kingsway, and interconnected into the BBC ring main system.

On Christmas Day 1932 the BBC linked up the British Empire, in a first historic occasion when Christmas messages of peace and goodwill were relayed, starting from London with the chimes of Big Ben and going from station to station right round the world, in a demonstration of unity and comradeship which overcame distance and time in a manner which astonished the world of the 1930s. At that time, when travel was so much more difficult, it seemed amazing that, whilst Britain was enduring a cold winter day, South Africa was sweltering under a hot summer afternoon, in India it was eight in the evening, in Australia it was a mid-summer midnight and in parts of Canada it was a frozen dawn. The hour-long link-up passed from territory to territory, with each country adding its own contribution and all united in the Spirit of Christmas. The hour terminated with the chimes of Big Ben, and as the great bell struck 3 p.m. the voice of HM King George V was heard from his home in Sandringham, speaking to his peoples scattered all round the globe. Truly it was an occasion when the motto of the BBC, 'Nation Shall Speak Peace Unto Nation', came to life, and the mellow notes and music of the bells of Big Ben will be always linked with these messages of peace and friendship.

From that time on, the sound of Big Ben was always used with all Christmas broadcasts and on all occasions of national importance, to herald great tidings of joy or sorrow. With the introduction of the Empire Broadcasting Service it was so greatly appreciated that it was employed on a regular basis instead of the time signal – indeed it did become 'the Signature Tune of the British Empire' and even when the Empire Broadcasting Service had made way for the World Service, the demand from all over the world was such that the sound of the bells is still played far more frequently on this service than in the United Kingdom. And in far-off New Zealand a record of the sound of these bells used to be played before every meeting of their Parliament.

Twenty-six years after Big Ben started broadcasting, cameras were mounted on St Thomas's Hospital and at 11.59 on 31 December 1949 the face of the great clock accompanied the chimes in ringing out the Old Year and the deep notes of Big Ben in ringing in the New Year of 1950. Since then this well-loved face has been featured on news and current affairs programmes almost every day – sometimes many times a day, accompanied, where appropriately and timely, by the music of the bells. It has become by far the best known as well as the best loved face on British television screens and is widely used to represent Britain on the television of almost all nations of the world.

The very idea of a New Year without the face of Big Ben as well as the sound of the bells is now almost unthinkable, but the presentation of an adequate picture has always had its problems. This is because during the winter the floodlighting of the clocktower is cut off at 11 p.m. Although the dial lights remain on all night, a picture of a dial with back illumination only would be less than artistic and inappropriate to the occasion, giving the impression of a silhouette portrait without a frame, which would negate the usual cheery warmth of Big Ben's face on the television screen. The Independent Broadcasting Authority have frequently used recordings of both the sound and the vision of Big Ben, but the BBC have prided themselves on the fact that the tones of the great clock are always 'live'. To meet this difficulty the BBC have created a model of the clockface (with some advice on detail and lighting from the Resident Engineer) and have used it for their New Year programmes with the assistance of 'live' sound from Big Ben.

The great clock has always played an important part in the Remembrance Day Ceremonies, held at the Cenotaph in the presence of Her Majesty the Queen on the appropriate Sunday in November and broadcast 'live' to the nation on radio and television and to other countries by satellite link and on the World Service. The chimes before the hour prepare everyone for the two minutes' silence which starts at the first stroke of Big Ben for eleven o'clock. To ensure absolute synchronism of the strike of Big Ben with the guns which sound at both the start and the end of the silence, an Army Signals Unit is accommodated in the clockroom on the morning of the ceremony, to send radio signals for the precise time for the gunners in the park to be absolutely accurate. To aid the television presentation, it has been customary, for many years, for a special runway to be built on the roof of one of the Parliamentary buildings opposite the Cenotaph to enable one of the TV cameras, which are transmitting the ceremony, to be run back to show close-up pictures of the north and east faces of Big Ben at the crucial times. In 1983, however, the clocktower was shrouded as part of the general cleaning programme of the Palace of Westminster, and only the east face of the clock was visible from the Cenotaph through an aperture in the cladding. This meant that only a long-distance view of the face could be shown on the screen.

Big Ben has been featured on the cinema screen for a longer time even than its sixty years as a broadcaster. Initially it was often shown on the silent screen to indicate that the action of the film was to be in central London. With the introduction of the 'talkies', the sound of the bells, already famous over the radio, was added to the visual image and became a regular feature of the newsreels. Even after the cinema newsreels had passed into antiquity, Big Ben has still retained its attraction to film directors and is still featured in many major productions. Requests for permission to film action scenes in the clockroom have to be turned down with regularity. Where possible, however, some help has been given in allowing pictures to be taken which can be used with back projection in studio reconstructions. These were used to some effect in *The Thirty Nine Steps* but its idea of an actor hanging on to the hands of Big Ben cannot be other than fantasy.

Big Ben has even entered the popular world of records, being incorporated irst in Eric Coates, *Knightsbridge Suite*.

The clock has always been a godsend to cartoonists and is incorporated in one guise or another in cartoons throughout the world in every week of the year.

The Big Ben bell has not only sounded joyously, but been used as a symbol to signify the nation's grief. It was first used in this way on 17 May 1910 when the clock was silenced at 11 a.m. and Big Ben was tolled whilst the body of King Edward VII was brought from Buckingham Palace to lie in state in Westminster Hall, and again when the coffin left for Windsor.

Similar action was taken for the funerals of King George V in 1936 and King George VI in 1952.

On the day of Sir Winston Churchill's funeral the bells were silent from 9.45 a.m. until midnight.

15 Summer Time

He that will not apply new remedies must expect new evils; for time is the greatest innovator.

F. Bacon, 'On Innovations'

The inscription on the base of 'Little Ben' in Victoria apologizes for the introduction of British Summer Time, but to the custodians of the Great Clock, and indeed to the clock itself, it was an innovation which provided the opportunity to have certain maintenance work undertaken with the least inconvenience to Parliament and the general public. It has always been the practice to do as much maintenance work as possible whilst the clock is running but some tasks can be undertaken only whilst the mechanism is stationary.

It is, of course, relatively easy to advance the hands one hour, without stopping the clock, but the hands must never be driven backwards, and so, like any other clock, Big Ben must be stopped in the autumn to return to Greenwich Mean Time, commonly known to all non-Service people as GMT; the Armed Services call it Z (Zulu) time and call British Summer Time (BST) A (Alpha) time and West German Time B (Beta) time.

The Daylight Saving Act of 1916, was a First World War measure to gain more production for the war effort, by inducing people to get up earlier in the morning during the summer months, but from this there arose the requirement to advance the clocks one hour in the spring and to set them back one hour in the autumn. In practice it has been the custom, since 1916, always to stop the Great Clock at the occasion of the time change in both spring and autumn.

Any stoppage of Big Ben has always been, 'news' to the

newspapers of the world, and even when it is the regular arrangement for the change-over to or from British Summer Time, it is necessary to send a message to the Press Agency to ensure that they have not forgotten and come out with big headlines 'Big Ben Stopped'. Even then many of the papers like to have some article on the Great Clock or on someone who is involved. The Press would very much like to be present, with their cameras, in the clockroom on such occasions, but as it is usually the only chance of doing really important maintenance work – such as changing worn bell ropes, re-packing and re-aligning bearings, re-dressing bell hammers and all the other tasks which can only be done when the clock mechanism is at rest – it has always been the rule that no one should be allowed to provide any distraction from the important work to be undertaken in the limited time available. The only exception to this rule of exclusion was made in 1982, when, at a time of minimum necessary work, with the agreement of the Speaker, permission to attend the change-over was awarded as first prize of a big charity draw.

The work to be undertaken at this time is normally carried out by four or five members of the term clock-maintenance contractors (at present Messrs Thwaites & Reed, the long-established firm of clockmakers whose offer to construct the clock had been unsuccessful), usually including one or more of the directors of the company, and the Resident Engineer of the Palace of Westminster. Most of the time is spent on intensive remedial work, but after midnight there is usually time to stop for a few minutes to drink coffee.

Over the years the procedures have changed a little but the basic drill is very much as set out below:

The Great Clock is allowed to chime at 9.45 p.m. on the Saturday night and then the lights behind the four dials are extinguished and the clock is stopped by placing a bar on the frame running through the gravity escape wheel.

The chiming and striking bells are disconnected by fitting shackles on the bell ropes. The hands of the clock are then advanced to the twelve o'clock position – the dials remaining dark. This is done by opening the legs of the escapement (with the bar temporarily removed) and allowing the 'going' mechanism to drive all the hands directly. This alignment of the hands is made to avoid confusion to anyone able to see them against a darkened dial, and to have them ready for starting later. The position of the hands is controlled manually from the indication shown on the sixty-minute wheel, which is duplicated at the back of the clock, near the escapement, where it can be seen by the man who is opening the legs of the escapement.

The pendulum is allowed to swing freely throughout this period of maintenance and adjustment, unless any work should be necessary either to it or to the pendulum cock (which would be most unusual). The energy stored in the pendulum is sufficient to keep it swinging freely for many hours, but should some unusual work prolong the work beyond the usual time, it may need a small hand push to restore it to its full motion before the clock recommences.

The maintenance work then proceeds and, in the normal way, all is programmed to be complete for the going train and the hands by midnight as would be reckoned on the new time.

At midnight (GMT or BST as appropriate) the clock is restarted and allowed to drive the hands at the new time. As this new time is not then official, the dial lights are kept off, and chiming and striking are kept disconnected until the new time is introduced at 2 a.m. During this period several checks on the accuracy of the timekeeping are made and any corrections adjusted by adding or subtracting pennies or halfpennies to the boss of the pendulum. A further full inspection of the going train, in action, is made and maintenance work on the chiming and the striking trains, and on the bells, is allowed to continue for a further hour and a half, should this be necessary.

At approximately 1.50 a.m. on the new time for the Sunday morning, the work of reconnecting the chiming and striking trains to their bells begins with the removal of the shackles from the bell ropes. At 1.59 a.m. the dial lights are switched on from the Engineering Control Room and the chimes start ringing in time for Big Ben to strike 2 a.m. to bring in the new time officially and to be back in full operation again.

This general procedure is kept much the same in both spring and autumn, although the period of maintenance is necessarily curtailed in the springtime, when the hands are advanced an hour, reducing the time available for work.

For the benefit of those particularly interested in the

The Clockroom on 5 August 1976

The shattered mechanism

The chiming drum

Mr R. Parish and other Harwell Scientists testing the
mechanism for cracks and flaws

The great bell under overhaul

Bells from above

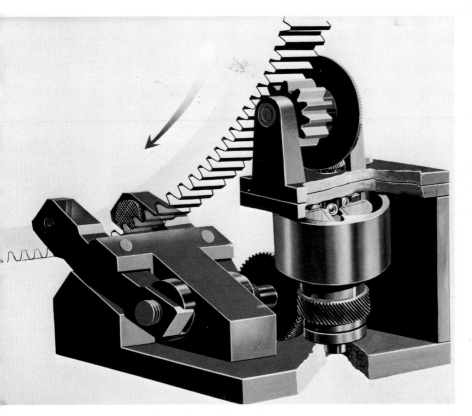

The 'fail-safe' mechanism

The cleaning of the Clocktower

maintenance of the Great Clock, a section is included in Appendix IV, outlining some of the problems involved in its history.

16   The Centenary of Big Ben

'Father Time is not always a hard parent, and though he tarries
for none of his children, often lays his hand lightly on those who
have used him well.'

C. Dickens, *Barnaby Rudge*

As the clock struck eleven on the morning of 3 June 1959, a
ceremony to commemorate the centenary of Big Ben began
in New Palace Yard. The Speaker and his chaplain, the Lord
Chancellor, the Prime Minister, the Leaders of the Labour
and Liberal Parties, the Lord Chamberlain and the Minister
of Works took their seats on the platform; also present at the
ceremony were Members of both Houses of Parliament and
representatives of organizations connected with the study and
making of clocks and bells.

At the last stroke of eleven o'clock the Speaker's chaplain
read the prayers, which included the following:

Let us thank God for them who in generations past dedicated
their gifts of design and skill and industry to raise aloft this tower
and therein to set up this Bell. Thanks be to God.

Let us give thanks that, surviving the dangers of war, to
ever-widening circles across the world this Bell has sounded
forth; symbol of stability in time of peril, symbol of unity in time
of peace, recalling day by day the great traditions which we have
inherited in this place. Thanks be to God.

[*Response*] From generation to generation.

Let us pray for the whole company of those who in our
generation hear this voice.

Following the prayer and the Grace, Mr Speaker addressed
the assembly:

My Lords, Ladies and Gentlemen,
We have met to celebrate the hundredth anniversary of Big Ben. The name is properly applied to the great bell which strikes the hour; so called after Sir Benjamin Hall, Mr Molson's predecessor in office a century ago. We are glad to see among us today Major Monteith, the great-grandson of Sir Benjamin Hall, the original 'Big Ben'. By popular usage the name has come to be used not only for the bell but also for the clock.

The Great Clock is somewhat like our Parliamentary Constitution in that, though it was born in controversy and wrangling, yet it keeps excellent time and serves us admirably. It was designed by that (sometimes irascible) genius, Mr Denison QC, later Lord Grimthorpe. The clock mechanism, exclusive of the bells, weighs five tons: so it is not the kind of timepiece that a man wears on his wrist. The central feature of the mechanism is the escapement devised by Denison and now known to horologists, the world over, as the 'Grimthorpe double, three-legged, gravity escapement' – a standard feature now of most great public clocks. It may be noticed that this escapement is double like our bi-cameral Parliament, that it is three-legged, like the 'Three Estates of the Realm'. Furthermore, that it relies on gravity, or the pull of mother earth, for its correcting influence – mundane, practical and thoroughly British. It works.

This contrivance of Denison's has a certain great merit. External influences such as wind-pressure on the fourteen-foot-long minute hand, are not communicated to the pendulum. No matter what gales may rage up there, the pendulum, with a bob of four hundredweights at the end of its thirteen-foot shaft, beats its two-second swing unconcernedly, unaffected by what is happening outside. Exact time is thus maintained. Human beings cannot maintain the impassivity of bronze or iron, but it is not inappropriate to say that in all the storms of the centuries that have beat upon us, the pulse of our Parliament has maintained a certain steadiness and regularity or 'Order' in its proceedings.

After much contention, the manufacture of the clock was entrusted to Mr Dent, a famous clock-maker of the time. The firm which he founded has maintained the clock, under contract, over the century. The extraordinary accuracy of this purely mechanical clock is a remarkable tribute to their zeal and care and also to the skill of the Victorian workmen who cut the gearwheels and other parts with implements of the time and to their successors who have carried on the good work. I am glad to see here Mr D. P. Buckney, the Chairman and Managing Director of the firm. He is the great-grandson of the original Mr Dent, the original clockmaker.

Big Ben proper, the great hour-bell, had a genesis as stormy as the clock. The first bell cast broke when struck by its ponderous hammer. It was recast into a new bell which now hangs in the tower. The new bell, too, cracked when struck with the heavy hammer. The crack was expertly treated, the bell given a quarter-turn, so that the blow should fall at right angles to the weak part, the weight of the hammer reduced to four hundredweights and this is the great bell we hear today.

Not only we. Thanks to the invention of wireless and the British Broadcasting Corporation, the voice of the great bell is now heard all over the inhabited earth. It was during the last war that the sound of its strokes attained a peculiar poignancy, especially during the time when we stood alone. No doubt Big Ben sounded somewhat differently to those that loved us and to those who hated us. To our friends in all countries it was reassuring. Even though at times there were the background noises of sirens and the gunfire of our artillery, its punctual boom said that neither Big Ben nor the nation was put off its stroke by those things. To those who were bent on our destruction I think it sounded otherwise.

It may be that the microphone, being so near the bell, picked up imperfections, such as the crack. Microphones are very revealing. It may be that the technical difficulties of broadcasting at that time, when wavelengths had to be synchronized, led to some distortion in the sound received. It seemed to me, in any case, in those days, when I heard the great 13½ tons of metal struck by the four-hundredweight hammer, that the bell gave forth a harsh roar of defiance and, thereafter, a long reverberating growl, menacing ultimate destruction to our enemies.

Now Big Ben sounds down to us his mellow E Natural, the voice of peace and good will. So may he sound to our children's children, generation after generation.

Following his address Mr Speaker presented to the Minister of Works a wooden replica of the inscription placed on the stone at the base of the clocktower to commemorate the ceremony for the centenary; this replica is now on the wall of the clockroom, where it may be seen by visitors. The platform party was then conducted to the Jewel Tower of the Palace of Westminster where there was a centenary exhibition of the history of Big Ben.

The many models on show as part of this exhibition included one of the original models of the clocktower made by James Mabey, one of the stonecarvers who worked under Sir

Charles Barry on the beautifying of the Palace. Another model, which was specially made for the exhibition by Major F. B. Cowen and Mr F. West of the British Horological Institute, was specially marked 'Please Touch' as it represented a working demonstration of the 'Grimthorpe double three-legged gravity escapement' as originally devised for the Great Clock. Other displays included the boxwood patterns used for the casting of the great gearwheels and other parts of the mechanism and a number of highly enlarged photographs of Lord Grimthorpe, Mr E. Dent, Mrs Elizabeth Dent, Sir George Airy, the Astronomer Royal, and Sir Benjamin Hall, the First Commissioner at the time the clock was completed.

As part of the centenary celebrations the orb and shower of stars on the tip of the clocktower steeple (sometimes erroneously called the orb and cross) were floodlit with special projector lamps for the first time. Previous floodlighting could not throw light to this height.

LITTLE BIG BEN

In view of the continual public interest in the Great Clock, over so many years, it is not surprising that a large number of working models have been made and that many of them are still in use. Some of the earlier ones have become quite valuable antiques, with a ten-foot model being sold at Christie's in January 1982 for £1,728.

One of the most notable cast-iron ones, known as 'Little Big Ben', was erected adjacent to London's Victoria Station in 1892, where for many years it served as a useful guide to many hurrying to catch trains. After seventy-two years service it fell into disrepair, and it was taken down in 1964 when road alterations were proposed. Its absence was deeply felt by many of those who used Victoria Station. In response to requests, the miniature clocktower was re-instated on 15 December 1981 by the Westminster City Council with the help of Elf Aquitaine UK, who assisted in the rehabilitation of the structure and the fitting of a new electric clock movement, as a gesture of Franco-British friendship. It is located on one of the new traffic islands created by the re-routing of the roads.

In addition to the plaque recording the assistance given in

the rehabilitation of the clock, there is the following inscription:

Little Ben's Apology for Summer Time

My Hands you may retard or advance.
My Heart beats true for England as for France   JWR

This clocktower, which stands some fifteen feet high, is surmounted by a weathercock. The actual cast-iron tower, although decorative, was never designed to be an exact replica of the Big Ben Tower, and the four clock faces were never as ornamental as those designed by Pugin on the original. The new faces are larger in diameter and much clearer than the older ones and are very brilliantly illuminated. The electric clock mechanism does not chime or strike the hours.

This symbol of Franco-British friendship had an earlier predecessor when the British community in Argentina put up a stone clocktower of similar design in the name of Anglo-Argentine friendship in Buenos Aires, to celebrate the independence of the country. Unfortunately, following the expulsion of the invading army from the Falkland Islands, the clocktower was set on fire; maybe it will be rehabilitated in years to come.

There are many other replicas in various parts of the world. A memorable, if transient, one was Big Ben in ice, some twenty feet high, which was built in Japan. A recent addition of a scale working model of Big Ben with a clock with the chimes and hour bell has been installed in the Children's Village near Klagenfurt in Austria.

17   The Great Catastrophe

And Time a maniac scattering Dust,
And Life a Fury slinging flame.
          Tennyson, 'In Memoriam'

The greatest catastrophe in the long life of the Great Clock
came 'like a bolt from the blue', with no warning or any visible
weakness which might presage trouble to come.

The first sign that there was anything strange came at
approximately 3.45 a.m. in the morning of 5 August 1976 and
was noted by the policeman on duty at the south-east corner
of New Palace Yard, almost a hundred yards from the foot of
the clocktower. He heard an unusual sound which he later
described as a kind of muffled boom which echoed in the
vaulted arches of the colonnade which runs along the east side
of the Yard. He walked along but could see nothing unusual
in the dim gas lighting of the Yard – the floodlighting of the
Clocktower had been switched off at midnight, as usual, and as
neither House was sitting there was no Ayrton Light. He
noted that the clock faces shone out with their accustomed
brilliance. He walked through the arches into Speaker's
Green, which was illuminated only by the lights on Westminster Bridge, seeing nothing strange, and from there back to his
post through Speaker's Court, wondering whether the noise
he had heard had come from something on the Victoria
Embankment or perhaps from Whitehall. It was only when he
had returned to his post that he noticed that the Great Clock
had stopped. He then, as required in the standing orders for
any difficulty affecting the building, phoned the Engineer's
Control Room to tell them that Big Ben had stopped and
added that he had heard a loud, muffled boom.

The Control Room of the Palace of Westminster is located

in a mezzanine floor built into the side of the Chamber of the House of Commons and is normally manned by relays of Control Engineers, twenty-four hours a day, whether the Houses are sitting or not, as the Palace is always busy and this is the focal point for all emergencies, other than security, in all the buildings occupied by Parliament. Among a host of other controls which operate the multitude of services, it houses the periscope through the viewing end of which the Control Engineer can see into the Commons Chamber and so can take early action to deal with any emergency or take anticipatory action to adjust the environment to meet the sudden changes which occur when there is an unexpected Division and the occupation of the Chamber changes from a mere dozen to some six hundred in a matter of a few minutes.

The Control Engineer had arrived for duty at 11 p.m. on 4 August 1976, expecting to have a quiet midnight watch, and he was looking forward to enjoying the tranquillity as a complete change from the previous week. Both Houses had just adjourned for the long summer recess and, as is usual in the week before, there had been a number of all-night sittings and a burst of last-minute activities. Now both Chambers were silent, the committee rooms were empty, the many dining-rooms and all the bars were closed, the kitchens were unattended, the libraries were locked up and even the Members' rooms were vacated. The corridors were empty apart from the patrolling custodians, and the eighty lifts were still. The lighting attendant had made his rounds to see that all unnecessary lights throughout the Palace had been extinguished, and had returned to report that all was well.

When at about ten to four in the early morning the policeman from New Palace Yard telephoned to say that Big Ben had stopped and that he had heard a mysterious noise, the Control Engineer thought that possibly one of the weight ropes had parted, stopping the clock, and that it had been the sound of the weight thudding down onto the sandbags at the base of the tower which had been the noise heard. Having phoned the BBC to let them know that Big Ben was out of action and that they would need to use the Greenwich Pips for the Time Signal on the World Service, he took up his torch and the keys and set off for the base of the clocktower to investigate. He did not hurry in climbing up the nearly three hundred steps to the clockroom as he expected that there was little that he would be able to do to get the clock going. He thought his task would be to see what appeared to be wrong and to inform the clock maintenance contractors, Thwaites & Reed, so that when they came in from St Leonards-on-Sea, as urgently as possible, they might bring the correct equipment to renew the cable which he assumed had been broken.

When he reached the upper landing and unlocked the clockroom door, he received what was perhaps the greatest shock in his life. The scene of devastation before him was almost beyond belief. The clock mechanism was a heap of wreckage lying over the ruins of the broken frame which had collapsed between the piers which had previously supported it. The floor was almost knee-deep with broken gearwheels and shafts; the walls and ceiling were scarred and pitted with metal fragments as if a shrapnel shell had exploded in the room, and there were several larger holes in the ceiling where larger pieces of metal had been driven through. The Control Engineer could only conclude that a bomb had been detonated under the main frame of the clock with dire results. In accordance with general instructions, he touched nothing and left the clockroom immediately, locking the door behind him. He rushed down to the telephone on the floor below and dialled his mate in the Control Room, asking him to call in the Bomb Squad from nearby Cannon Row police station. He then went down to open the lower doors at the foot of the tower to admit the Bomb Squad on their arrival.

The Bomb Squad arrived very quickly, took the keys of the clockroom and belfry and slowly climbed the tower. When they saw the clock mechanism, they were amazed at the utter devastation but quickly dismissed any idea that the damage could have been caused by a bomb. They soon decided that, although the windows had been pierced and smashed by metal fragments, none of them had been blown out, as would have happened if there had been a sudden rise in the pressure in the room such as would have been caused had there been an explosion in the room. After a very thorough search of the clockroom and belfry and the other rooms in the tower, they concluded that all the destruction in the clockroom had been due to mechanical failure which had given rise to a massive release of energy which had wrecked the mechanism.

The immediate risk of further damage or danger to the building being lifted, the District Works Officer and the Resident Engineer were notified and Thwaites & Reed called in from their works at St Leonards-on-Sea. It was decided that, before any detailed investigation or repair work was undertaken, it was important to have a full record of the havoc in the clockroom by having proper photographs taken before anything was moved. The Department of the Environment official photographer was summoned from the Elephant & Castle and arrived early to take many detailed photographs of the damage (Plates XIII to XV). Action was also taken to inform the serjeant at Arms, and he advised the Speaker, and also the Chairman of the Accommodation and Administration Sub Committee, Mr Robert Cooke MP.

18 The Incredible Damage

With ruin upon ruin, rout on rout,
Confusion worse confounded.
Milton, *Paradise Lost*

The extent of the damage, covering so much of the clock-room, was such that it tended to make one think that the whole of the mechanism was ruined beyond redemption. But after some short period of mental adjustment it was possible to close one's mind to the overall devastation and give detailed examination to each individual 'train' of the complex systems and to realize that there was the hope of salvaging something from the colossal wreck. Although there had been a collapse of the whole mechanism, and the 'going train' and the 'striking train' had both crashed down and been partly covered by the flying debris, it appeared possible that some parts of these might be recoverable and that the major devastation had been caused to the 'chiming train' which was located on the right-hand side of the mechanism.

In fact, the whole of the 'chiming train' with all its massive and complex mechanism had virtually disintegrated, leaving an empty space on the wreck of the now broken bedplate on which it had been located. The enormous chiming drum, complete with its ratchet drum, cams and gearwheels, the whole weighing more than half a ton, had been thrown into the air, shedding pieces of gearwheel, castings and clicks (ratchet pawls) in all directions. This main drum had been flung across the clockroom to crash into the wall before coming down on the heavy timber bench below, which smashed to fragments; this did something to cushion the impact and prevent the drum rolling further and doing even more damage. It was indeed fortunate that the clockroom wall was nearly three feet thick, so that it was able to contain the inertia of the drum. Had this wall been weaker, the drum might have been driven right through and, at the height it was, it would have continued through the glass of the dial to crash to the ground some 180 feet below.

The main frame of the clock mechanism, which is fifteen feet long, had been fractured in five places and, instead of bridging the space between the two masonry piers, the broken bedplate, still holding the damaged striking and going trains but without the chiming train, which had completely disintegrated, was resting on the top of the partially crushed winding motor. The giant flyfan (air brake) of the chiming train was broken off a few feet above the earlier level of the mechanism and, with its bevel wheels shattered, lay across the gantry supporting the drive to the hands. Virtually all the mechanism at this end of the clock was smashed and scattered over the clockroom floor in small pieces. The white walls of the room had been peppered with metal fragments as if from a fragmentation bomb. Heavier pieces of gearing, weighing up to ten pounds, had been driven clean through the thick timber ceiling and were later found in the lever room above. The chiming weights (1¼ tons) had fallen to the base of the tower but much of the energy of their fall had been dispersed in wrecking the chiming mechanism, and the remainder was absorbed by the sandbags at the bottom of the weight shaft, with only some minor damage to the pulley.

The going and striking trains had both been extensively damaged by flying metal. The celebrated Denison double three-legged gravity escapement was so badly twisted that it was rendered useless; the going drum and its arbor (shaft) were so mutilated that they would need to be replaced. The striking train had suffered less, although there was considerable damage due to flying metal.

Most fortunately the pendulum cock and the pendulum itself, though so close to the damaged escapement, were unharmed, although fairly large fragments of metal were found in the pendulum pit. The main part of the pendulum was of course sheltered by the cast-iron pendulum pit, whose only open part was the slot at the top in which the pendulum rod oscillates. It was a remarkable feature of the metal storm in the clockroom that these sizeable fragments found their way through the narrow slit into the pendulum pit.

Altogether the damage appeared so extensive that it seemed doubtful if the Great Clock could ever be completely repaired. It would have been very easy to have done nothing at the time. But the minds of those involved could not conceive of Britain without Big Ben, and all started to put in hand the initial work of clearing up the mess and examining the possibilities of repair. Despite the enormous devastation, there was a glimmer of hope that it might just be possible to get some part of the mechanism in working order again, even temporarily, as an indication that ultimate repairs were possible.

The greatest of good fortune was that the pendulum and the pendulum cock were unharmed, and next to this was the chance that the clockroom held a spare escapement. Many years ago the original escapement had been damaged and replaced. The old one had been repaired and had been kept as a spare. Could this good fortune presage the possibility that the clock might work again? It was, of course, appreciated that the whole of the chiming train would have to be replaced, and that this, with the many hundreds of special castings and fabricated parts, would take many months at the best, and probably even years. But could there be a possibility that the clock might be made to work without chiming? To Britain and the world, Big Ben without the chimes was inconceivable, but to London and Parliament the faces of the Great Clock showing the accurate time were of special importance.

Everybody went into action with deep devotion to clear away the wreckage and to clean up all the rough edges and other damage to the going train caused by flying metal. Bearings were eased and shafts were re-aligned. It was not possible to straighten the arbor of the going drum or to repair the drum itself, but by adjustment to the bearings it was possible for this part of the train to function in a satisfactory manner for the period of months which it would take to replace these items. The damaged escapement was removed by John Vernon of Thwaites & Reed, and he carefully installed the original one, which had been refurbished so long ago in preparation for some emergency then unexpected. In the meantime the DOE/PSA scaffolder, Frank Harris, and his mate were rigging tackle and toiling up the three hundred steps to the clockroom carrying two heavy-duty jacks, each capable of raising a load of three tons, which were carefully edged under the broken bedplate of the clock mechanism. Very slowly, inch by inch, the broken frame, still carrying the damaged going and striking trains, was eased back into the horizontal. The possibility of providing some rigid support for this section of the frame was considered, but in view of the fact that the weight, even without the chiming train, would have been almost four tons, it was not deemed practical and it was decided to leave it standing on the two jacks.

After all possible checks and adjustments had been made, it was decided to try to start the clock. The pendulum was given a gentle touch to bring it to full amplitude and the escapement engaged. All held their breath and waited, and then came the deep, solemn tick, resounding through the clockroom, almost like a sound of triumph as Big Ben took up, once more, his age-old duties of driving his hands around the four great dials. Shortly after 4 p.m. on 5 August 1976, less than thirteen hours after the great catastrophe which had wrecked half the mechanism, Big Ben was again telling the time with its customary accuracy.

Big Ben had triumphed once more. To have got the Great Clock back into service again, on the same day, after such a catastrophe, was a tribute not only to the Victorian designers, engineers and craftsmen who had built it so well but also to the devotion of their counterparts of today. Perhaps the greatest triumph lay in the fact that Big Ben could inspire such determination and devotion.

It would have been possible for the great bell of Big Ben to have sounded out that afternoon (although, of course, without the music of the chimes to precede it), but it was decided to keep the bell silent, whilst further tests were made on the striking train. This train was so similar to the chiming train that there was always the possibility that the fault, which had caused such devastation when it occurred on the chiming train, might be duplicated on the striking train. Big Ben was therefore silent for the next eleven days, and Great Tom of St Paul's took over the radio duties.

19 The Seeds of Disaster

'Time will reveal everything.'
Euripides (480–406 BC)

The vast release of energy which had caused such havoc could only have come from the great weights of the chiming system. It was roughly calculated that the potential energy stored in the 1¼ ton weights of the chiming train must have been equivalent to almost half a million foot-pounds force, and this could have been released only by the weights running out of control.

The governor of the system is the flyfan; this consists of large sheets of metal clamped onto the top of the eight-foot-long flyfan arbor (shaft) which rises from the driving bevel gears on the mechanism to its top bearing and ratchet, which are anchored to the ceiling of the clockroom. The area of these two fan blades aggregates some twenty-five square feet, and the rotation of the flyfan moves a quantity of air and so acts as an air brake to control the speed of rotation of the chiming drum and so controls the release of energy to the bells to ensure that they maintain the correct intervals between the strokes. If for any reason the air brake failed to control the speed of the train of gears, it was possible for the weights to take charge and rotate the chiming drum at an increasing speed so that the mechanism could run wild.

Attention was therefore directed to the flyfan, but it was found that this appeared to be in good order apart from some slight damage from the impact of its fall. The flyfan arbor, however, showed a failure about three feet above the cast-iron bevel wheels, which were also fractured; the failure had the appearance of a tear in the hollow metal shaft. This arbor,

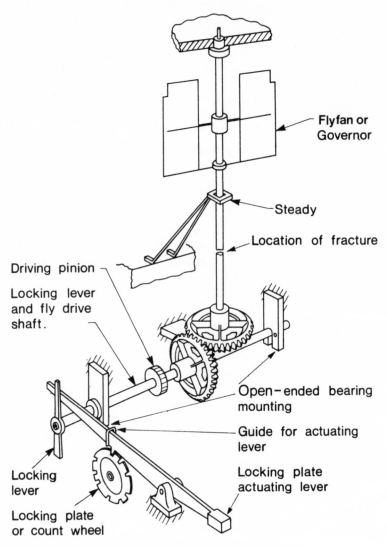

Flyfan or Governor

Steady

Location of fracture

Driving pinion

Locking lever and fly drive shaft.

Open-ended bearing mounting

Guide for actuating lever

Locking lever

Locking plate actuating lever

Locking plate or count wheel

4   Arrangement of Locking and Fly Mechanism

which was the one originally fitted during the construction of the clock, had been made by the practice current in the nineteenth century for lightly loaded shafts, by taking a sheet of wrought iron and rolling it into a tube, with the long seam hammer-welded by a blacksmith. The National Physical Laboratory (NPL) were called in from Teddington the next day and took away the broken flyfan arbor and the bevel wheels for examination in their laboratories. As it was suspected that the similar arbor on the striking train might also be vulnerable, and for this reason the striking of the hours had been suspended, it had also been dismantled and prepared for the NPL to take away for examination.

Following a very detailed examination the NPL reported that the fracture in the flyfan arbor had been due to metal fatigue in the wrought iron starting from the hammer-welded seam. This definitely confirmed what had been surmised: that the whole catastrophe was caused by the fatigue failure of this hollow shaft, approximately one inch in diameter, which the NPL reckoned had been twisted some four million times in the last 117 years.

The confirmation of this cause of the disaster immediately focused attention on the similar flyfan arbor of the striking train, which had been sent to the laboratories for examination. The NPL reported by telephone that they had examined the external surface of this shaft minutely and could see no fault. They then asked if they could cut the hollow shaft to be able to see if there were any internal cracks. The Resident Engineer, who had already taken the precaution of ordering a replacement arbor to be made of seamless steel, gave his permission immediately.

A few days later the NPL reported that, after cutting the tube, they had found fatigue cracks, similar to those in the flyfan arbor of the chiming train, starting from the inside and penetrating three quarters of the way through the thickness of the metal. From this it might be supposed that the cracks on the chiming arbor might not have been visible to normal inspection methods from the outside prior to the failure, and that under normal practice it would have been virtually impossible to prevent. It also meant that a similar catastrophe might well have been likely to the striking train within the next decade, had not a new arbor been provided.

In the urgent endeavours following the catastrophe, all attention was directed to locating the seat of the troubles, to repair the clock mechanism as far as this was feasible and to take all possible steps to ensure that Big Ben would continue to function with safety and reliability for the benefit of future generations. During this anxious time there was little leisure to ponder on the seeds of the disaster.

Later, when there was more time to think of fundamentals, there came to mind the question as to why such men of genius as Denison and Dent had ever designed their masterpiece, the clock, to have these vulnerable flyfans so far removed from the precious mechanism, which they were intended to control and protect. Considering their vital functions, surely it would have been wiser to have incorporated them solidly within the framework or at least rigidly attached to the bedplate, instead of having them fed by long, spindly shafts away aloft near the ceiling of the clockroom?

For centuries the traditional position of the flyfans of turret clocks had been for the fans to be built into the framework of the mechanism with the arbors horizontal and driven by simple gearing. Of course, the flyfans for the Great Clock needed to be vastly larger than those on any earlier mechanism, but all the same it might have been possible to have them mounted on some back or side extension to the basic frame. By such an arrangement the fans would have been smaller, as they could have rotated faster, and would have been inherently more stable, as they would have been mounted on shorter arbors, firmly fixed between rigid bearings securely anchored to the frame. Such an arrangement, with the flyfans mounted horizontally behind the bedplate proper, was adopted in the clock which Denison designed for St Paul's Cathedral and which was made by John Smith of Derby. So why was not such a time-honoured and very sound system adopted for the Great Clock?

Surely the answers to these questions lie deep in the very virulent antagonism existing between the Architect of the New Palace of Westminster and the Clockmakers, which had direct repercussions on the design of the clock when the historic visit to the clocktower took place on 22 March 1852, when the Astronomer Royal, Denison and Dent met Barry. At that time the clocktower was only about half its final height but when they all expressed dismay at the space available for the mechanism, it was made very clear that, although some additional space could be provided, a major change, such as would be required to meet the designs of Denison and Dent, was out of the question. Unfortunately no documentary evidence can be found of the discussions but it can be surmised that the factor which upset all Denison's designs was the hollow central airshaft which formed the structural core of the tower. Although this had by this time reached a height of only some 120 feet, Barry felt it absolutely essential for the structural strength of the tower for it to continue centrally through the space between the clockfaces which had to contain the clockroom. This meant that it was quite impossible for the flyfans to be accommodated in the designed position behind the bedplate. It also meant that the access from the only staircase of the tower prevented Denison's locating the flyfans at the ends of the bedplate, whilst the necessity for room to wind the clock by hand prevented their being positioned in front of the mechanism.

Had relationships been more amicable, it might have been possible for the structural designs to have been modified, even at this late stage, to carry the structural strength through the strong walls of the surround of the clockroom, or perhaps to have started the heavy structural cast-iron members, which now begin at the belfry, immediately above, from the clockroom level. But under the circumstances such compromises were impossible.

There is little doubt that Denison and Dent spent many worried months considering how to get this great mechanism into the space available. Indeed, this was the cause of the quarrel between Denison and Airy, which led to the Astronomer Royal to tender his resignation to the Chief Commissioner of Works in November 1853. In the long run Denison decided that the only course open to him was to take the flyfans up vertically to the ceiling, and so unwittingly he sowed the seeds of all the troubles that were to occur some 123 years later.

20 Investigation: To Repair or to Replace?

Once to every man and nation comes the moment to decide.
J. R. Lowell

Following the re-starting of the Great Clock on the afternoon of the day of the catastrophe, a discussion was held in the clockroom with Mr (later Sir Robert) Cooke MP, Chairman of the Accommodation and Administration Sub Committee of the House of Commons, Mr H. Rogers, Assistant Director London Region DOE/PSA, Mr B. Copson, Area Officer, and the District Works Officer and Resident Engineer. Also present was Mr G. Buggins MBE, Managing Director of Thwaites & Reed, the clock maintenance contractor.

The need for the full restoration of the Great Clock at the earliest possible date was most strongly urged by Mr Cooke. He stressed the special importance of Big Ben as the symbol of Britain throughout the world; as well as its being such an integral part of the House of Commons, it was also a priceless antique and a unique example of the genius of the great Victorians. Mr Buggins advised that his firm had the facilities for undertaking the massive work of repair and reconstruction, but he estimated that it would take at least fifteen months, until October 1977, to complete the task.

Mr Cooke reminded everyone that Her Majesty the Queen would be visiting her Royal Palace of Westminster on 4 May 1977 to receive the Loyal Address of both of her Houses of Parliament on the happy occasion of her Silver Jubilee. His Committee would consider it most important that all the bells should be chiming on this joyous occasion. The Resident Engineer felt that, if there were no further unforeseen difficulties, and with the full co-operation of all concerned, it might just be possible to meet this date. In his view, to achieve early completion of the repairs it was desirable to have a target date, and this important occasion should be accepted a the date to which efforts should be aimed. No firm decision arose from this meeting, as it was necessary to investigate, in depth, the possibilities that further damage had been caused to the mechanism.

Although the root cause of the great catastrophe had been discovered, the results of the tests carried out by the National Physical Laboratories on the unmarked flyfan arbor of the striking train caused deep concern. The arbor had been replaced by a seamless steel tube, and this enabled Big Ben to resume striking the hours from the middle of August 1976, but the finding of cracks and metal fatigue in what had appeared to be a flawless shaft made the Resident Engineer wonder whether other vital components, of the same age, could also hold invisible cracks, radiating from the inside, which might fail without warning. There was now no doubt of the damage possible from the great potential energy stored in the weights, and the latent possibilities for further destruction or even injury could readily be conceived.

A minute visual inspection of the important components had shown virtually nothing, and it was quite out of the question to contemplate cutting components for internal examination in the way the arbor had been cut. Most of the other items were castings which would take weeks or even months to replace. And the great question arose as to whether it would be practicable to repair the clock, wonderful antique as it was, if unsuspected weaknesses made such repairs a fruitless waste of money and effort. It was essential to have a deep technological examination by specialists who could look inside the metals of the mechanism without damaging or weakening the unique nature of the clock.

After much consideration the Resident Engineer approached the Non-Destructive Testing Section of the United Kingdom Atomic Energy Research Establishment at Harwell to ascertain if they could undertake a complete crack detection investigation of the whole of the clock mechanism, without impairing the strength of the machine or greatly interfering with its operation. The response was encouraging: they were prepared not only to undertake the work as a consultancy service but to give full assurances that a deep and thorough investigation could be done with no damage to the mechanism. Furthermore, they would give the work high priority.

Permission was therefore sought to place a consultancy agreement with the Atomic Energy Research Establishment (AERE) for this work to be put in hand as urgently as possible. This did, however, take some delay, and by the time all arrangements had been put in hand it was early in October 1976. It was necessary for men to be available to do the dismantling and re-assembly of the mechanism as well as to do any small remedial work involved. There was at this time no contract left for the overall repair of the clock, as it was not known whether these tests would show that a repair was feasible, but the Resident Engineer still had the clock maintenance contract, on which it was possible to order this necessary attendance.

As it was now October, it was decided to avoid inconveniencing Members of Parliament and the general public by stopping the clock whilst the House was sitting, by taking special measures to extend the normal period of shut-down for the change-over from British Summer Time to Greenwich Mean Time on 23/24 October 1976. On such occasions it was usual to have a few hours for routine maintenance, but for this task the Speaker agreed that the stoppage could be from midday Saturday 23 until 8 p.m. on Sunday 24 October. For such occurrences it was always necessary to notify the Press and Broadcasters well in advance, otherwise the headlines of papers throughout the world would feature a stoppage of Big Ben. Even with this warning both the Press and television took the greatest detailed interest in the work being undertaken that weekend.

The time available was, of course, insufficient for all the testing work which was essential, but it was possible for many of the static areas to be crack-detected whilst the clock was still working. The Harwell scientists, under their manager Mr Ron Parish, started on Monday 18 October to lug their heavy equipment up to the clockroom, where they carried out such tests as were possible on items which were static for at least an hour at a time, during the period up to Saturday morning. The conditions of working, up there high in the clocktower, were far from ideal, but they managed to get through many of the more accessible tasks. After the clock was stopped at midday on Saturday, they worked continuously night and day until the task was complete at eight o'clock on Sunday night. Throughout all this work Mr John Vernon, Technical Director of Thwaites & Reed, and his men worked alongside the Harwell men, dismantling the parts for examination, cutting out cracks to their roots, making simple replacements and reassembling the mechanism. During the earlier part of the week, before the clock was stopped, the co-operation of these two groups was perfected, and when the all-out effort at the weekend was required their integration, inspired by devotion to Big Ben, was beyond praise.

Various types of crack-detection procedures were used on different areas of the mechanism. The everyday methods of normal radiography could not be applied, due to the impossibility of taking the heavy X-ray equipment required for the deep penetration up the clocktower. In place of this an Isotope Iridium 192 source was proposed for gamma ray penetration of most of the deep castings. This in itself posed some problems, as it had to be contained in a thick lead encasement which was tremendously heavy to take up the tower. An arrangement of blocks and tackle was mounted on a temporary beam across the stairwell by the DOE scaffolder, and this helped tremendously, although there was still much manhandling required as, for safety sake, this isotope had to be kept in a room on the floor below and only brought up for each specific task, when every possible precaution was taken.

Magnetic particle examination was found to be very effective with the use of fluorescent inks and ultra-violet light. Ultra-sonic testing was used mainly to examine the long bolts and to gauge the thickness of items which were difficult to dismantle. Full use was also made of the older techniques of visual inspection, using such simpler penetrants as paraffin and chalk.

At 5 a.m. on Sunday morning 24 October 1976, the tests showed up serious cracks in the pair of bevel gears which drove the striking flyfan arbor. These gearwheels were of cast iron, and both were showing internal cracks. This was most serious as a failure of these gears could have released the air-braking control and caused a disaster to the striking train similar to that which had wrecked the chiming train, and indeed most of the clock, in August. As an immediate precaution the Resident Engineer instructed that the striking of the Great Clock be suspended once more. So Big Ben, which had been striking the hours, without the chimes, since the middle of August was silent once more. This naturally caused great interest in the media, and the Resident Engineer had to explain the causes of the further difficulties on television programmes which were shown worldwide.

In consideration of the great importance of the clock as an antique, it had been intended that all repairs to the mechanism should be reconstructed in the same or very similar metals to preserve the historic appearance of the clock. Here, however, it was felt that safety was paramount, and the Resident Engineer considered that the integrity of the mechanism for future generations justified a change in the material of these vital gearwheels from cast iron to gunmetal, in the same way as he had changed the metal of the flyshaft arbors from wrought iron to seamless steel. The difference in this case was that, although the arbors looked identical, the gearwheels would change from a cast-iron grey to a gunmetal colour. The toughness of gunmetal would, however, ensure that these bevelwheels would last for hundreds of years, and, as gunmetal had for many years been a traditional material for the construction of old clocks, it would not distract from the overall appearance of the mechanism. After the completion of the testing on that Sunday night, an order was placed on Thwaites & Reed to have a new set of bevelgears made in gunmetal, and Mr John Vernon took the cracked ones with him back to St Leonards. The new ones were quickly made and machined so that the striking of Big Ben was resumed at noon on Monday 1 November 1976.

A large number of other flaws and cracks were detected in the careful examination, but only three in the bevelgears lever and locking lever were considered serious. The locking lever was also replaced, as a failure of this in operation could cause damage. It is interesting to note that many of the flaws and blowholes shown up by the non-destructive techniques were original faults in manufacture, and many of them had been carefully filled with putty and painted over to have lain unsuspected under their paint for so very many years. However, as these were not in any vital or heavily stressed areas, and as they had withstood 117 years of constant working, including the enormous shock of the catastrophe, without strain it was considered safe to leave them alone. All the minor cracks on the working parts were cut out to the roots and 'pop marked' with a centre punch to enable them to be kept under observation; this was to ensure that further action could be taken if there were signs in future years of any of the cracks starting to grow once more.

One series of cracks which merited rather special attention were those in the great camwheel of the striking train. Although a possible failure in this area would not pose any serious hazard, it was in a highly stressed region as the cams on this wheel had to transmit the full force of the action to strike the four-hundredweight hammer of the Big Ben bell. As these cracks were fairly deep, it was decided to make and shrink on a special reinforcing ring.

Taking into account all the many cracks and flaws which had been uncovered by this exhaustive enquiry, it was apparent in the cold light of reason that the Great Clock was fundamentally sound and repairs were possible.

Nevertheless, the decision whether to repair or replace was a complex one. In terms of sheer economics there was not a great deal to choose. The replacement of the chiming mechanism more or less completely would involve a great deal of special design work. There were many complicated castings to be made both for the chiming train and for the repair of the frame and all the rest of the damaged pieces; although there were a number of patterns which had been preserved from the 1959 Big Ben Exhibition, unfortunately few covered the area destroyed. The production of drawings, patterns and castings and the subsequent machining would prove expensive.

The cost of reconstructing the mechanism was likely to be about three-quarters of that of providing a modern electric or hydraulic movement of equal reliability. The question then arose as to how long such an electric system could last. Big Ben had provided impeccable service for 117 years, and it was confidently predicted by all the authorities that, after repair, the minimum extra life of the clock would be at least a hundred years – indeed, with increased care and periodic attention from some modern system of non-destructive testing, it seemed likely that the mechanism could easily go on for another two hundred years. The possibility of any electrical system lasting even a quarter of that time could only be a matter of speculation. Another important factor in the consideration was the undoubted fact that the Great Clock was a priceless antique and a landmark in the history of horological science. Quite apart from this, there was the fact that Big Ben was deeply beloved by people not only in Britain but also from all over the world, and letters were pouring in showing their real anxiety and even offering to help restore Big Ben to its rightful place in the BBC World Service.

Although some Members of Parliament thought this might be a suitable time to install a new and modern system in the Great Clock, it was notable that most of these had never ventured to scale the tower to see the wonderful old mechanism at work. The House of Commons Accommodation and Administration Committee, under the chairmanship of Sir Robert Cooke, was particularly concerned that, if at all possible, the clock mechanism should be preserved, retaining as much of the original material and appearance of the great machine as was practicable, and this recommendation was subsequently ratified by the Services Committee. The Civil Service branches concerned were sympathetic to the idea of the restoration but felt that all practical alternatives should be explored.

Discussions were held with a number of prominent clock-manufacturers on the possibilities of repair or replacement, and full consideration was given to a number of alternative designs and proposed modifications which might seem worth while. On closer examination, however, it appeared that all of them would have serious limitations, and none of them seemed to offer the degree of reliability that could be expected from a full reconstruction of the original mechanism. None of the very few firms willing to reconstruct the existing mechanism was prepared to give a fixed price for the work, or to promise to meet the target date of 4 May 1977. This was quite understandable, in view of the real difficulties which could be foreseen in the coupling-up of an alternative system to the mechanism of the hands on the four great dials.

The basic decision was therefore taken that full repairs should be put in hand, although it was recognized that, with the unforeseen delays already incurred due to the essential crack-detection, the target date appeared unattainable.

21 The Brave Endeavour

A brave endeavour,
To do thy duty, what e're its worth
Is better than life with love forever,
And love is the sweetest thing on earth.

J. J. Roche

After nearly three months delay occasioned by the essential testing, the possibility of completing the repairs to the mechanism to have the bells chiming for the arrival of Her Majesty on 4 May 1977 had been abandoned by most of those concerned. Yet it still remained feasible in the mind of the Resident Engineer, who believed that devotion to Big Ben could work miracles, especially when working through the agency of Mr John Vernon of Thwaites & Reed. But there were many more difficulties, still unforeseen, to overcome before the work could go full steam ahead.

Whilst the crack investigations were being arranged and conducted, a full search was being made at the Public Record Office for drawings of the Great Clock, as any which might have been lodged in the Resident Engineer's Office would have been destroyed when the House of Commons was destroyed by the bomb in 1941. As none were found at the Record Office, it was suggested that they had been sent to the Royal Observatory, Greenwich. Some of the relevant papers were eventually traced to the Maritime Museum, Greenwich, but unfortunately all of them related to early design sketches and details of schemes put forward in other tenders. Nothing useful was found, and it would appear from later examination of Lord Grimthorpe's papers that it was doubtful if any 'As Fitted' drawings of the mechanism were ever made. The only reasonably accurate sketch which could be found was the small line drawing in the frontispiece of Lord Grimthorpe's book *A Rudimentary Treatise on Clocks, Watches and Bells*, third edition (Fig. VIII). Unfortunately this was very much a diagram and gave few dimensions and nothing which could be of any use in the reconstruction of shattered components. Furthermore, it was found by direct observation that such details as the number of teeth on the various gearwheels did not always correspond with those which were actually on the clock. It must be remembered that at that period much was left to the individual craftsman, who was not always bound to work exactly to the information given.

It was therefore necessary to build the chiming gear more or less from scratch, with very little design information, and largely working from the shattered remains of those parts which could be pieced together. Fortunately there were some of the original wooden patterns which could be reused for some castings, but regrettably these did not include much of the chiming train, and the most intricate patterns for the larger castings were missing.

Endeavours to get the work in hand in time to meet the target date were now beset with very serious contractural difficulties. As none of the firm of reputable clockmakers was prepared to tender a firm price for the repairs, but all insisted it must be a cost-plus-profit contract, there were distinct advantages in placing the work with Thwaites & Reed, who had already been helpful in getting the clock going on the day of the failure. Apart from their deep knowledge of the clock which they had maintained for the last six years, they held the term maintenance contract which included a schedule of rates which had been let in open competition. Although there were many tasks involved in these major repairs which were outside this schedule, it was at least a basis on which negotiations could take place. The Resident Engineer therefore recommended that an agreement be let with Thwaites & Reed on this basis.

Unfortunately the Contracts Division of the Department of the Environment, Property Services Agency, who would let the contract, were greatly concerned because there were strong market rumours of the financial instability of the firm, which was going through a bad patch, and they thought the firm might be going out of business. Contracts Division, who were most sympathetic, pointed out that it would be unwise to let the task to a firm which would be unable to finish the task, as the Great Clock might be in trouble for many months – indeed, there might be the greatest trouble in getting it finished at all. They agreed that from an engineering and even an economic viewpoint Thwaites & Reed appeared to be the best answer, but from a financial angle it would be wise to wait a few months to see if the firm was stable, and in the meantime make further enquiries.

The Resident Engineer, who had fully explored the market for an alternative repairer, felt that the firm had one priceless asset, Mr John Vernon, their Technical Director, who was an exceptionally competent craftworker on turret clocks. He had the real advantage of knowing the Great Clock like the back of his hand and had a deep devotion to Big Ben. He had given a personal assurance to the Resident Engineer that, if the worst happened and the firm were to close, he would be prepared to work with the Resident Engineer's staff and it would be possible to complete the work with the aid of some small contractors who could make the castings. There was also the consideration that the firm was less likely to close if it was known that they had been entrusted with the repair of Big Ben.

The advice from the Contracts Directorate to wait a few months was undoubtedly sound but these months were not available. The House of Commons Committee were most helpful and were giving all the support possible, but they were still pressing for the completion of the chiming bells for the Queen's visit on 4 May 1977. Even the BBC were pressing to know whether the chimes would be ready to let in the New Year of 1977 and, when told that this would not be possible, wished to know how long before they could meet the requirements of their listeners throughout the world. A further factor of considerable weight was that the Resident Engineer had considerable anxiety as the Great Clock mechanism was still running perched precariously on the two three-ton jacks pressed into service on the day of the catastrophe. Up to now Thwaites & Reed had been able to undertake all the preliminary and small remedial work on the maintenance contract, but now they were in the position of not being able to place the orders for the castings and other materials without an official instruction.

In these circumstances the Resident Engineer felt he must take a major risk to get the work in progress. He therefore took the unusual step of issuing an 'Instruction to Proceed' to Thwaites & Reed. This might have landed him in a great deal of trouble, but it did at least get the work of repairing the clock in production, and when they heard about it, the Contracts Division were most understanding of the difficult position which had arisen. With this instruction the work went ahead at good speed, although it was constantly dogged with financial difficulties which necessitated the Resident Engineer nursing along the sub-contractors to encourage them to complete their work, with the assurance that they would be paid.

A minor crisis arose when it transpired that the Managing Director had under-estimated the size of the task when he had assured the Committee that he had all the facilities to undertake the repair. Of course, Big Ben is still excessively large as far as clocks go, and no one should have been surprised that Thwaites & Reed had not got a lathe large enough to turn the castings. Unfortunately they could not hire one large enough, and this part of the work was at a standstill. The problem was, however, met by authorizing them to purchase a second-hand lathe of adequate size, against the contract, on the basis that it was to be sold, with the necessary credits, as soon as this part of the work was completed. The end of all these financial troubles came in March 1977, when the National Enterprise Board bought up the entire stockholding of Thwaites & Reed, which made it virtually a nationalized company. Most fortunately they decided to retain all key personnel, including Mr John Vernon. This removed all anxieties on the completion of the repairs and gave an additional stimulus to the work.

Although he still hoped to complete the work for the target date, the Resident Engineer, after much heart-searching, had decided he must put an additional constraint on the work, although he knew it must delay progress. The full report from the Atomic Energy Research Establishment had shown up so many flaws and blowholes in the original castings that it raised doubts as to whether the present-day castings being made by the sub-contractors might not be similarly flawed. The Resident Engineer therefore decided that it was necessary for every new casting and forging produced for the repair of the clock to be sent to the Non-Destructive Crack Detection Centre at AERE, Harwell, to be radiographed to ensure that it was free from flaws before it was machined. This decision involved some measure of delay, which was regrettable, but the wisdom of this move became apparent as seven pieces had to be rejected on account of flaws, and indeed the largest and most complex casting had to be made three times by the sub-contractor. As it was intended that the Great Clock should endure for at least a couple of centuries, it was essential that only the very best and most reliable components should be incorporated in the reconstruction.

Notwithstanding all these troubles and delays, the brave endeavour of reconstruction pressed on, and every visit to the factory at St Leonards-on-Sea showed good progress, so that it became possible to expect that the target date could be met after all.

The Commons Committee, together with the Antiquarian Horological Society and all the other friends of Big Ben were most anxious that the overall appearance of the great mechanism should be preserved, as far as possible, in order that generations to come should be able to see this great antique masterpiece looking as it did before the catastrophe. This was especially stressed by that distinguished antiquarian horologist Mr T. R. Robinson FBHI, who had written so much to the *Horological Journal* at the time of Big Ben's Centenary in 1959.

This desire was also in the mind of the Resident Engineer, although he was conscious of the difficulties which stood in the way of achieving this worthy intention. The obstacles were not so much in the re-creation of the mechanism – although here it was necessary to use more advanced metals in the more critical and highly stressed areas; with the sole exceptions of the flyfan bevel gears, where gunmetal was used, the stronger metals employed were identical in appearance with the originals.

It was in the region of the main frame of the clock that it was necessary to cut off the last five feet length of the bedplate, which had previously supported the chiming train, as it was so badly shattered that repairs were out of the question. It was, of course, possible to make a substitute section of the bed-plate of the highest grade cast iron, on which the reconstructed chiming train could sit; it was even possible to match up the lettering of the long inscription which had been on the bedplate since it was made in 1854, in such a way that it was continuous. The major difficulty concerned the way in which it was to be bolted onto the remainder of the frame.

The bedplate of the machine had carried the full weight of the mechanism, some five tons, as a bridge between the two masonry piers, but with a join in the middle of the frame it was no longer possible to carry this weight without additional supports. It might have been possible to provide an inconspicuous prop at the back of the mechanism had all the connection been possible there, but of course the joint had to be at the front (in the most noticeable part of the front too!) as well as at the back, and the props needed to be substantial rolled steel joists. It was foreseen that this would be difficult because of the problems which had arisen to frustrate the provision of temporary props to avoid leaving the mechanism standing perched on the two three-ton jacks for all these months.

The greatest difficulty was that the floor of the clockroom was not strong enough to take the weight of the supports which would have to be located at the joints of the new and the old frames. The maintenance surveyors of the London Region of the Property Services Agency of the Department of the Environment were called in to undertake the difficult task of designing the necessary steel reinforcement to the floor. In this they were handicapped by the Resident Engineer's requirement that nothing must show. They did an excellent job in designing three stout girders in the very confined space, two of which had to run along the length of the bed and the other across the bed cut into the stout walls of the air shaft which went right down to the foundations of the tower. Unfortunately the presence of other beams and reinforcing members so restricted the space that it was not possible to conceal the crossbeam completely below the floor level and, although the cement had been graded up to meet the top of this girder, it was impossible to hide the slight bulge in the floor at this spot. However, with the new vertical girder painted black to match the frame, very few of the people who knew the clock well in the days before the catastrophe have ever noticed the alteration.

22 The Last Lap

To the last syllable of recorded time.
Shakespeare, *Macbeth*

By the middle of March 1977 all the new castings had passed their radiographic tests at Harwell and had been machined with accuracy at Thwaites & Reed's Works at St Leonards-on-Sea; only the making of some minor pieces remained for the completion of the manufacturing work. Thanks to the devoted work of the staff and employees of the company, their suppliers and sub-contractors, and the testing staff at Harwell, who had given such priority and long hours to the work for the Great Clock, it now appeared that the target date, which had once seemed impossible, was in sight of being achieved.

To mark the virtual completion of the manufacturing work, Mr G. Buggins MBE, the Managing Director, and the officials of the National Enterprise Board held a small ceremony in the factory on 26 March 1977, with the main items of the new chiming train mounted up in the new portion of the bedplate. The guest of honour on this occasion was Professor F. G. Smith FRS, who was at that time Director of the Royal Greenwich Observatory at Hurstmonceaux and who is now the Astronomer Royal. This was a welcome continuation of the historic connection between Big Ben and the Royal Observatory, and a reminder of the part played by the then Astronomer Royal, Sir George Airy, and Edmund Beckett Denison (Lord Grimthorpe) in the design of the Great Clock.

Following the ceremony and demonstration, the smaller remaining items were completed and the main components were dismantled and divided into suitable parts so that they could readily be transported up the clocktower in April 1977.

The work of reconstruction on site began early in April and progressed as far as possible without disturbing the running of the Great Clock, which was still perched precariously on the two jacks. At the request of the Resident Engineer, the Speaker of the House of Commons kindly agreed to the Great Clock being stopped for the last week of April to enable the crucial final stages of reconstruction to proceed. Notwithstanding all the preparations which had been made, there was still a vast amount of work which could be done only in the short period whilst the clock was stopped. Furthermore, all of it had to be done perfectly, as this was the very last week before the Royal Visit.

With the clock being stopped, it was possible to tackle the intricate task of fixing the new chiming-train section of the bedplate onto the pedestal and lining it up to marry with the old remaining frame. In addition to perfect alignment it was important for the sake of the appearance of the mechanism that the new cast-iron letters of the long inscription (see page 161) to be completely in harmony and continuous with those on the original part. After the weight of the frame had been taken by the new vertical stanchion, it was possible to bolt it all up solidly and to remove the two jacks which had given such yeoman service in providing the support that had enabled the clock to function for the past eight months.

There were now complex tasks to be performed on the chiming train, including the new locking plate and locking arm, installing all the cams and ratchet gear, winding the ropes on the great chiming drum and connecting the pulley, anchor and weights, and running and connecting the five ropes which operate the hammers on the four chiming bells; there were also a number of tasks to undertake on other parts of the mechanism.

It will be recalled that the winding of the going mechanism had been badly damaged and its arbor had been bent on the day of the catastrophe. This was a truly vital sector as the drum provides the motive power for the running of the clock. Temporary repairs had been cobbled up on the day in the effort to get the clock working once more, and it had not been possible to replace these items since then as it would have involved stopping the clock for a considerable time whilst the going train was dismantled. Fortunately the temporary repairs had been adequate to keep the hands moving and the pendulum swinging throughout the period. The complete replacement of the drum and its arbor during this shutdown ensured that the going train would be in first-class condition for centuries to come. This and other modifications to the old mechanism did involve a number of problems. All the new gearing had, of course, been machine-cut and was uniform throughout the circumference and could mate with the corresponding pinion at any point. The old gearing was, however, hand-cut and by no means uniform, so that it would mate with other gearwheels at only one designated point; if they were assembled even one tooth out, they would eventually jam and the clock would stop. This did lead to some 'teething troubles' in the re-assembly of the mechanism.

A rigorous system of tests was carried out with the bell shackles anchored so that the behaviour of all parts of the chiming train could be tried out and adjusted to perfection over the full range of the chimes for a simulated twenty-four hour day with the bells silent. Eventually, on the Saturday afternoon, all appeared satisfactory and the final paintwork was applied so that the clock mechanism would look as much like its old self before the disaster took place as possible.

23 The Ultimate Triumph

'There must be a beginning of any great matter, but the continuing unto the end, until it be thoroughly finished yields the true glory.'

Sir Francis Drake's Prayer

Although the full array of silent tests had been satisfactory, and the bells and their hammer gear had been overhauled by specialist sub-contractors during the months when they were silent, it was most desirable that the range of the chimes be tested audibly, before the special day. The Resident Engineer approached the Speaker of the House of Commons, through the Serjeant at Arms, and it was agreed that full tests, including the ringing of the chimes for a series of tests, might be undertaken on the Sunday immediately before the Royal Visit; it was hoped that the unusual testing of the bells on this Sunday would attract little public attention, especially as the bells of Westminster Abbey would be pealing at about the same time.

It was expected that the testing of the bells would be only a last-minute formality, and only Mr John Vernon of Thwaites & Reed and the Resident Engineer were to be present. In fact, it was fortunate that it was undertaken, as a slight distortion in the sound of the bells was detected which appeared to affect the sweet music of the chimes. The sound of the chimes in the belfry is subtly different to the sounds heard at ground level, due to the echoes and diffusion of the sound through the ornamental stonework of the clocktower, so efforts to trace the source of this distortion involved climbing up and down the clocktower several times to check on the various adjustments which were being made, which was very arduous on account of the 340 steps. Eventually the trouble was traced to friction in the lever room above the clockroom, where the cables from the chiming train pass through a number of cranks to reposition the cables so that they are directly below the appropriate bell. It was friction in these cranks, which had been out of service since the day of the catastrophe. The cranks were gently eased and relubricated, and this cured the difficulty, although it involved a further journey up and down the clocktower to make sure that the sound was really to the complete perfection expected from Big Ben. (Unfortunately the Resident Engineer, who was temperamentally inclined to hurry on the ascent, had a heart attack on this last climb, but he had the satisfaction of knowing that all was well for the Royal Visit.) Afterwards the BBC made detailed comparisons between the sound of the chimes against tapes made for record purposes prior to the catastrophe, and even 'the golden ears of the BBC' declared the sounds identical.

On 4 May 1977 Her Majesty the Queen drove to her Royal Palace of Westminster to celebrate, with great pageantry, the Silver Jubilee of her accession to the throne. The ceremony was held in the time-honoured Westminster Hall, the scene of so many royal occasions in nearly a thousand years of British history.

As Her Majesty and HRH the Duke of Edinburgh entered the hall at noon, the chimes of Big Ben rang out, clearly and joyously, for the first time for nearly nine months, followed by the twelve deep strokes from the great bell. As the sounds were dying away, a fanfare arose from the full array of the State Trumpeters, attired in their colourful tabards, high up beneath the north window of the hall.

Her Majesty took her seat before an assembly which included HM Queen Elizabeth the Queen Mother, HRH the Prince of Wales and most of the royal family as well as a full array of the Lords and Commons of her Parliament. The Loyal Address on behalf of the House of Lords was read by the Lord Chancellor, the Rt. Hon. the Lord Elwyn-Jones, and a further Loyal Address on behalf of the House of Commons was read by the Speaker, the Rt. Hon. George Thomas PC (now Viscount Tonypandy). The Queen graciously replied, and the whole assembly rose to give a spontaneous 'Three Cheers for Her Majesty'.

It was a tremendous occasion and, thanks to the devotion of many, Big Ben had triumphed once more! How delighted all who had worked on the creation and repair of the Great Clock, over the years, would be to know that Big Ben's loyal and joyous greeting was the first heard on this historic occasion.

The Resident Engineer, recovering from his serious heart attack in the intensive care ward of the nearby Westminster Hospital, heard the chimes from his bed and rejoiced. The nurses very kindly brought in a television set so that he could see and hear the historic ceremony at which he should have been present.

24   Safeguarding the Future of Big Ben

Time present and time past,
Are both perhaps present in time future,
And time future contained in time past.
                                    T. S. Eliot

People of all nations had shown such an affection for Big Ben when it was out of action that it was essential to take all possible measures to ensure that the catastrophe should never re-occur and that the Great Clock be fully safeguarded as a legacy to generations to come for many hundred years.

The public concern, shown by many letters of enquiry from all parts of the world, included offers of practical help and even of money if it would do something to restore the beloved chimes. To meet this demand for information the Resident Engineer had to be interviewed on a multitude of radio and television programmes in many countries.

In addition, to meet the wishes of Parliament, it was decided to mount an exhibition in Westminster Hall (one of the very few exhibitions ever allowed in this hallowed hall) at which the story of the catastrophe was told in words and pictures, with some of the larger fractured items on display. This was a success and was seen by more than thirty thousand people in this location alone and subsequently shown at many centres in Britain. Word of it went to Australia, and such was the demand that the Australians shipped the exhibition out by air to New South Wales where it was very popular. Although it was shown only in New South Wales, as it was urgently required back in Britain, there were enquiries from other places. Some months later the Resident Engineer received a scroll with ribbons and a large seal from Brisbane (which was not visited by the exhibition) nominating him 'Favourite Listener for 1977' for 'Restoring to the Australian People the Sound of Big Ben'.

The very deep concern shown by the peoples of not only this country but throughout the world indicated that special efforts should be made for the preservation of this master-piece of Victorian horology. One of the lessons learnt from the catastrophe was that the safeguarding of this precious heritage should not be left to the thrice-weekly inspections and minor maintenance undertaken at the time of winding the clock, and to the twice-a-year maintenance periods, which were of brief duration whilst changing the times, and covered visual inspections and the periodic changing of ropes etc. As the weaknesses found in the mechanism had not been detect-able by visual examination, it was necessary to supplement these earlier routines by periodic non-destructive crack de-tection to give early warning of any possible future trouble.

As an additional safeguard, to prevent any substantial damage being done to the mechanism or the clocktower by a possible future massive failure, it was decided to commission the National Physical Laboratory (NPL) to design and build a device which could operate to ensure the safety of the clock and its surroundings, by the mechanism 'running away' should there be a sudden breakage of one of the flyfans or bevel gears. The NPL were keenly interested in this commis-sion as it involved new lines of investigation, breaking new ground on the boundaries of science and engineering. There was also the possibility that the device which might be evolved would have applications in other branches of engineering.

The Resident Engineer, in arranging this commission, felt it necessary to impose two conditions. The first was the most important, and the most arduous. It was essential that any new system be completely reliable and not prone to accidental operation. He therefore requested that 'the device must be more reliable than the Great Clock'; in this it was accepted that he was demanding the impossible, for what could be more reliable than Big Ben had proved to be over 117 years? But this served to clear the mind as it led to the quick rejection of the basis of many of the schemes first mooted. The second condition was much easier, in that it simply required that any device should be so concealed within the mechanism that it did not detract from the historical appearance of the mechanism.

After many months of deep thought and many experiments, a system was invented by Mr J. E. Furze and Mr N. B. Owen at the NPL whereby the initial energy released by the weights when they started to run away was harnessed by the device to apply disc brakes to bear on one of the great gearwheels to slow it down and bring the rotation of the massive winding drum to a speedy halt. It was an ingenious device by which a pinion engaged with one of the existing gearwheels rotates a ball clutch. At the normal speed of rotation for chiming, the ball is held down by gravity and the clutch does not engage. If the rotation is faster than normal, the ball is thrown out by centrifugal force and the clutch engages the drive to a screw thread. This screw thread as it rotates tightens the disc brakes on either side of the wheel (Plate XIX) and brings the mechanism to rest.

The device was tested many times in the laboratories, in the presence of the Resident Engineer, and was judged reliable. It was installed on the chiming train of the Great Clock during a maintenance period whilst the clock was being changed from Greenwich to British Summer Time. Full tests were carried out with the chiming weights lowered in the weight shaft until they were only nine inches above the sandbags at the base of the tower. This was to ensure that very little damage would occur if the device failed to work and the weights ran wild. With only nine inches to run, they could do little damage. But the new system worked very well and halted the arranged runaway in less than four inches.

About five weeks later, however, this device, which had been provisionally called 'the fail-safe device', operated when the chiming was performing in a perfectly normal way and the mechanism was completely safe. This was on an afternoon when the House of Commons was sitting, and although it did not stop the clock, or the striking of the hours, it did tie up the chiming completely.

As many of the Members in the Chamber of the Commons below rely on hearing the quarter bells, for the timing of their remarks, it was essential that the chimes be restored as urgently as possible, without the delay involved in bringing in men from Thwaites & Reed at St Leonard's-on-Sea or the

National Physical Laboratories at Teddington. As the hands and the striking were continuing normally, the release of the chiming gear from the false operation of the fail-safe device appeared a straightforward matter. The Resident Engineer, after sending a message to the Speaker explaining the position, collected one of the Control Engineers and climbed up the three hundred steps to the clockroom, to try to release the chimes by removing the device whilst the clock was working. This proved more difficult than was expected, as the NPL had used metric bolts (on an antique clock!) with recessed heads which required a special box spanner which was not available. When it was freed, it was necessary for the Resident Engineer to operate the locking bar manually to bring the chimes back on schedule by allowing the bells to chime three times in immediate succession, which was most embarrassing with the House of Commons listening below! One could almost imagine Big Ben chuckling to himself, in minor triumph, 'Did you expect this new-fangled device to be as reliable as I am?'

The trouble was due to the ball clutch reacting to vibrations from the clock mechanism. During all the laboratory tests the possibility of the device being affected by vibration had not been considered, and the short-duration tests undertaken in the restricted period of the change-over from Summer Time did not permit the phenomenon to be apparent. What had happened was that the vibrations set up by the release of the heavy levers for the striking of the bells had caused the ball in the clutch to escape and slowly mount the groove so that it was in effect on a hair trigger and ready to operate as soon as the chiming wheels started to rotate, even at slow speed. The trouble was rectified by an alteration to the profile of the groove in the ball clutch. This was tried out on a vibration table in the laboratories at various speeds and with a range of frequencies of vibration before it was proved reliable at all combinations likely to occur. On being accepted as satisfactory it was re-installed and re-tested on the clock at the next time-change period. Since then there has been no trouble due to accidental operation of the device.

In March 1980 the Resident Engineer decided it was time to test the device once more during the change-over to Summer Time. Although the device worked and stopped the weights running away, it took a few seconds longer than before. This resulted in a drop of about six inches of the weights, in place of the four inches previously observed. This extra two inches might seem small where the potential drop of the weights is nearly 180 feet, but in fact it meant that the energy to be absorbed was at least twice as much as had been released in either of the earlier sets of tests. Unfortunately all this extra energy was not absorbed in the disc brakes, and it resulted in considerable hammering of the locking arm, the locking lever and the locking plate. Although this hammering was only of a second or two's duration, it was very considerable. To be hammered for even a second by a force with a ton and a quarter behind it falling six inches can do a great deal of damage. In this case it resulted in heavy burring on all three of these items in the locking system. This involved a difficult task in that all these items had to have their burrs filed off and the assembly trued up. These efforts took so long that it was not possible to complete them before it was time for the clock to be restarted, so that final adjustments and smoothing off had to be done in the very short intervals between the chiming of the quarter hours. This was a nuisance but the trial was deemed a success as it had demonstrated that the device would certainly have prevented substantial damage had there been a real failure of the mechanism.

Initially this fail-safe device was fitted only to the chiming train of the clock, which was considered the most vulnerable, until experience had ensured its reliability. In 1981 a similar device was fitted to the striking train. These safety measures cannot readily be seen when visiting the clockroom, as they have been concealed behind the gearwheels of the hand winding gear. On request, however, the guide will usually take an interested observer round to the end of the mechanism, adjacent to the brass plate which commemorates the reconstruction of the chiming gear, from which point the safety device can be seen. There was no need to fit a safety device on the going train as it has a much smaller weight (five hundredweights), and the designed arrangement by which the flyfan for this train is a compact addition to the escapement, which meant that it had none of the vulnerability imposed by long vertical shafts which were a weakness on the other trains.

These safety devices must, however, be considered the

very last line of defence of the clock against catastrophe, to be applied automatically when all other means of safeguarding it have failed. The main measures to keep the clock in good heart will always be constant vigilance in the regular routine inspections and preventative maintenance, supplemented by periodic non-destructive testing of all hazardous items to ensure that metal fatigue is not starting to weaken these members from the inside. Even with the use of such advanced technology, there have been some worries about the condition of certain parts which could not be reached for full examination.

Fortunately the most serious of these concerns, that of the condition of the hands and their central bearings, which have been inaccessible for the last 125 years, has now been lifted with the cleaning of the stonework of the whole Palace, including the clocktower. This work has now restored the beauty of what has been described as one of the architectural wonders of the world, and Big Ben, so long Britain's national symbol, will be seen in its full glory. This cleaning, with its necessary scaffolding, has enabled each of the four dials to be overhauled in turn while the clock continued working and showing the time on the other dials, with the bells sounding as usual. The radiographical examination of the hands, after their removal, found them in remarkably good condition, with only tiny hairline cracks in one or two of the central bosses, which were stopped. The opportunity was taken to renew the central bearings on which the hands were pivoted as these showed a small degree of wear. This action should ensure the smooth running of these very inaccessible parts, which should now be safe for at least a couple of centuries.

Big Ben has become such an accepted part of everyday living that perhaps it needed some great event to bring home to everyone what a very special place it occupies in their hearts and minds. It was unfortunate that the event came near to destroying this masterpiece of art and science. Although Big Ben was created in discord and bitter controversy, it has triumphed to symbolize stability, harmony, peace and freedom and to inspire worldwide devotion.

Big Ben is now in splendid condition, and its newly cleaned exterior reflects the inner care and attention which now surpass that given to any other clock. With the present standard of devoted care and the application of modern science to its preservation, there is every reason to expect that it will continue to operate, with distinction, for many centuries into the future and give pleasure and happiness to many generations of people.

Appendix I. The Astronomer Royal's Specifications 22 June 1846

I *Relating to Workmanlike Construction*
1. The clock-frame is to be of cast-iron, and of ample strength. Its parts are to be firmly bolted together. Where there are broad bearing surfaces, these surfaces are to be planed.
2. The wheels are to be of hard bell-metal, with steel spindles working in bell-metal bearings, and proper holes for oiling the bearings. The teeth of the wheels are to be cut to form on the epicycloidal principle.
3. The wheels are to be arranged that any one can be taken out without disturbing the others.
4. The pendulum pallets are to be jewelled.

II *Relating to the Accurate Going of the Clock*
5. The escapement is to be dead-beat, or something equally accurate, the recoil escapement being expressly excluded.
6. The pendulum is to be compensated.
7. The train of wheels is to have a remontoire* action, so constructed as not to interfere with the dead-beat principle of the escapement.
8. The clock to have a going fusee.**
9. It will be considered an advantage if the external minute hand has a discernible motion at certain definite seconds of time.
10. A spring apparatus is to be attached for accelerating the pendulum at pleasure during a few vibrations.

---

* A remontoire action is a device similar to that in the Airy Remontoire Dead Beat Escapement in which the maintaining power is independent of the weights.
** A going-fusee is a device described in Airy's paper to the Cambridge Philosophical Society on 2 March 1840 which keeps the going train working when the clock is being wound.

11. The striking machinery is to be so arranged that the first blow for each hour shall be accurate to a second in time.

III *Relating to the possible Galvanic Connection with Greenwich*
12. The striking detent is to have such parts that it can make or break a magneto-electric current.
13. Apparatus shall be provided in order to make it possible to convey the indications of the clock to several different places.

IV *Relating to General Reference to the Astronomer Royal*
14. The plans, before the commencement of the work, and the work when completed, are to be subjected to the approval of the Astronomer Royal.
15. In regard to items 5 to 11, the maker is recommended to study the construction of the Royal Exchange Clock.

[signed] G. B. Airy 22 June 1846.

Additional Condition added by the Astronomer Royal in February 1847

16. The hour wheel is to carry a ratchet-shape wheel or a succession of cams, which will break contact with a powerful magnet, at least as often as once a minute for the purpose of producing a magneto-electric current, that will regulate other clocks in the New Palace.

Appendix II. Facts and Figures

THE CLOCK TOWER

Height to the finial	316 ft
Height to the centre of the clock faces	184 ft
Height to the belfry	205 ft
Height to the Ayrton Light	250 ft
External size of the base of the tower	40 ft square
Steps up to the belfry	340 ft
Steps up to the clockroom	300

There is no lift up the clocktower.

THE CLOCK FACES

Number of faces	4
Diameter of the faces	23 ft
Number of panes of opal glass in each face	312
Length of figures on the dials	2 ft
Size of minute spots on the dials	1 ft square
Weight of each dial	4 tons

THE HANDS

Length of copper minute hand	14 ft
Length of gunmetal hour hand	9 ft
Weight of minute hand with counterbalances	224 lbs
Weight of hour hand with counterbalances	672 lbs

THE CLOCK MECHANISM

Length of bedplate	15 ft
Width of bedplate	4 ft 11in
Heigh of bedplate between webs	19 in
Weight on the pedestals	5 tons
Escapement Denison Double Three-Legged Gravity	18 in
Going train weight	560 lbs
Time to wind by hand	15 minutes

Striking train weight	1 ton
Time to wind by hand	4–5 hours
Time to wind by motor	30–40 minutes
Chiming Train Weight	1¼ tons
Time to wind by hand	4–5 hours
Time to wind by motor	30–40 minutes
Size of the winding motor	5 h.p.

THE PENDULUM

Length to the centre of gravity	13 ft
Overall length (top of spring to base of bob)	14 ft 5 in
Total weight	685 lbs
Weight of pendulum bob	448 lbs
Suspension spring: free length	5 in
thickness	1/64 in
width	3 in

THE BELLS

The great bell (Big Ben)

E Natural: Weight	13 tons 1219 lbs
Height	7 ft 6 in
Skirt diameter	9 ft
Thickness at sound bow	8¾ ins
Weight of hammer	448 lbs

The quarter bells (the chimes)

No. 1. G. Sharp: weight	1 ton 135 lbs
diameter	3 ft 9½ in
No. 2. F. Sharp: weight	1 ton 590 lbs
diameter	4 ft
No. 3. E Natural: weight	1 ton 1525 lbs
diameter	4 ft 6 in
No. 4. B Natural: weight	3 ton 1189 lbs
diameter	6 ft

The composition of the metal of the bells was designed to be 22 parts of copper to 7 parts of tin.

Appendix III. Winding The Great Clock

All of the three trains which form part of the mechanism of the Great Clock were designed for hand winding, and for the first fifty-four years there was no other method, so that it was necessary for two or three men to spend between five and six hours a day, three days a week, winding the clock by hand. This was very laborious work as the chiming weight was 1¼ tons and the striking weight was one ton, and each of them had to be lifted up to some 180 feet, depending on the period since they were last raised. Although the large two-man handles were connected to the winding drums by a train of gears, which meant that the handles were turned one hundred times for every turn of the great drum, they were still very heavy to turn. To wind either of the two drums from scratch would require some four thousand turns of the handle and would take approximately five to six hours. It would have been possible to wind these trains only twice a week, but it has always been considered important for sufficient stored energy to be kept available to meet any contingency, such as sickness or accident. It was also desirable that minor routine inspections and maintenance, including checking the accuracy of the clock and keeping a record of temperature and barometric pressure, be undertaken three times a week.

The going train, which moves the hands and controls the operation of the striking and chiming trains, has only a five-hundredweight mass to wind and has the capacity of running for about ten days between windings. Although it only takes about fifteen minutes to wind up this train completely on a single-man handle, it is still wound the small amount required three times a week along with the other trains. Power winding mechanism is now available, but it has always been normal practice to wind this train by hand. As with all accurate clocks it is essential to maintain power for the pendulum and the hands whilst winding is in progress, but in a clock of this size the problem is greater than that on most clocks where the winding takes only a moment or two. The device which Denison designed and had incorporated in the going mechanism for this purpose consists of a loose bar at the end of the winding arbor which hangs obliquely from the back pivot of the barrel and has a ratchet click on it which can engage in a set of ratchet teeth set in the back of the pass under the click, but as soon as winding begins, the bar is moved to engage the click. The great wheel then becomes the fulcrum, and power is transferred from the barrel to the great wheel directly. By this means the movement of the hands and the necessary impulses to the pendulum are maintained, even if the winding lasts as long as fifteen minutes.

On the striking and chiming trains the problem is much easier, as it is easy to stop winding, briefly, just before the time comes for the chimes, as indicated by the loud warning noise from the locking lever. The winding can then resume following the last sounds of the bells.

In 1912 Messrs Dent devised an electric winding system which was then powered by a five-horsepower direct-current electric motor. This machine has survived, and even withstood the impact of the mechanism falling on top of it in the catastrophe of 5 August 1976, although the direct current motor was changed for an alternating current one of similar size in 1970. This machine is still in regular use for winding the chiming and striking trains; it was designed to wind the going train also, but in this it has never been entirely satisfactory as it has been found to cause some irregularities. This has never been considered a matter of any importance by the maintenance contractors, who wind the clock, as handwinding takes only a maximum of fifteen minutes, and the practice of winding this train by hand is well established.

The procedure for winding the striking mechanism is a rather complex one but may be of some interest. It always starts immediately after the hour has struck as it usually takes between thirty and forty minutes to complete, and it is necessary to fit it in before it is time for the hour to strike again. As the winding days are normally Monday, Wednesday and Friday, the time taken on Monday is greater than the other days as the weights will have sunk lower after three days of working.

The normal winding drill for the mechanism is as follows:

After the hour has been struck, unhook the arm from the chain fixed to the frame and allow it to rest on the numbered wheel, noting the number engaged.

Release the dial on the winding machine from its pinion and set it to show the number noted at the three o'clock position (this number is normally one after the hour has struck). Wind up the dial mechanism and allow the dial to settle on its pinion.

Start the motor by the switch by the clockroom door which allows the drive to be taken up to the friction clutches.

Engage the left-hand friction clutch for the striking gear by lifting the weighted stop arm for the striking mechanism by raising the chain. It is important to release this chain and to ensure that it has not caught onto the stop catch. If this were to happen, the drum might overrun.

It is possible to engage the right-hand friction clutch in the same way for the chiming gear to be wound at the same time. If this is done, it is most important to stop the machine a minute before each quarter to allow the bells to chime.

After each barrel is fully wound and cuts out its friction clutch the motor is switched off. After it has stopped the weighted arms are to be hooked clear of the cams on the numbered wheel by the chain. The dial on the winding machine is then to be reset so that No. 13 (the neutral) is in the three o'clock position.

This completes the winding drill.

Appendix IV. The Maintenance of the Clock and Bells

The maintenance of the Great Clock, in accordance with the usual practice with other turret clocks, has always been entrusted to a specialist clockmaker, under the general supervision of the Resident Engineer of the Palace of Westminster. For 110 years this work was undertaken by the firm responsible for the original manufacture of the clock, Messrs E. Dent & Co., whose contract included the winding of the clock, the regulation and adjustment for accuracy, the oiling, the greasing and a regular programme of minor maintenance and inspections. They also undertook to provide an 'on-call' service, so that their men could be called out at any time, night or day, if there was trouble with the clock or bells. The contract also covered provision for them to undertake such major maintenance work as was required and specifically ordered. During this long period of their contract there were few stoppages, about thirty in all, most of which were caused by the carelessness of other workpeople in resting ladders against the mechanism or leaving paintpots in the wrong places. Apart from the major overhauls of 1934 and 1956, there would appear to have been only three or four occasions where stoppage was due to a failure of the mechanism.

The major overhaul in 1934, which necessitated Great Tom of St Paul's acting as substitute on the radio, was mainly for work on the bells, although the opportunity was taken to do some work on the mechanism. The Whitechapel Bell Co. (Mears) undertook the major work of renewing the hanging bolts of the bells and overhauling all the hammerwork, wire ropes and shackles on the quarter bells. Two of the quarter bells were turned to allow the hammers to strike new surfaces. The hammer of the Big Ben bell was dressed and the clapper, which had never been used, was cut from the centre of the inside of the bell to relieve the weight on the collar. It was left on the belfry floor below the bell as it could not be removed without lifting the Great Bell from its collar.

In 1956, when the clocktower was scaffolded for the repair of wartime damage, the opportunity was taken to do even more heavy work on the bells, and once more Great Tom had to deputize. For the first time since its installation, ninety-eight years previously, the Big Ben bell was removed from its suspension and the wrought-iron collar dis-assembled; the gudgeon pins were dressed and the loose clapper was removed and taken to its present resting place in the 'bandstand' immediately below the floor of the Central Lobby. Consideration was given to the advisability of turning the Great Bell once more, but it was decided that this might affect its tone, so it was replaced in its collar, with a large Hallite washer, in exactly the same position it had previously occupied, with the hammer beating on the same spot. The hammerwork was overhauled and the bosses on which the lever arm rested were built up by welding.

The four quarter bells were also lowered and their collars repaired, with the gudgeon pins replaced by stainless steel pieces. The bells were re-hung with white metal-asbestos joint washers in the boxes. All the hammerwork was sent back to the Whitechapel foundry to enable extensive repairs to be undertaken. New buffers, made of special rubber to avoid the trouble caused by the freezing of the earlier buffers, which had led to faulty chiming of the smaller bells in severe weather, were fitted and no further trouble was experienced until the severe weather of 1986 when trouble due to freezing of the rubber buffers was again experienced and replacement with silicon rubber was necessary. The opportunity was also taken of enclosing the belfry in wire mesh to avoid any further damage from pigeons.

In 1970 the firm of E. Dent & Co. were experiencing trouble in obtaining skilled clockworkers to replace the older men who had been maintaining the Great Clock and after much heart-searching asked to be relieved of the contract. It was put out to tender in 1971, with invitations going out to Gillett & Johnson of Croydon, Smiths of Derby and Thwaites

& Reed of Clerkenwell. Thwaites & Reed, an old-established firm that had built the clock on Westminster Abbey, were successful in obtaining the maintenance contract and, with some changes in ownership, hold it up to the present time.

The company (which more than a century earlier, had asked, rather late in the day, if they could tender for the original construction but had been refused by the then Commissioners) had always operated from Clerkenwell and with their local staff gave every satisfaction in taking over the maintenance contract. In the mid 1970s, however, they moved to St Leonard's-on-Sea, taking most of their key personnel with them. The facilities and staff which they had there were adequate and they were able to send over staff to undertake major maintenance work. They had left staff who were capable of winding and regulating the clock but were not able to carry out other duties. This meant that the 'on-call' requirements of the contract could not readily be met as each call out would have meant at least a two-hour delay. At one stage the firm made arrangements for a helicopter to be available to fly craftsmen to London. This would have saved only an hour at the most, but fortunately no emergency was sufficiently serious to justify this expense, after the system had been set up.

The position was eased in 1979, when the National Enterprise Board sold Thwaites & Reed, which they had acquired in 1977, to W. H. Elliott & Co., an old-established family firm of quality clockmakers. The new owners transferred the head offices of Thwaites & Reed to Croydon, from where they had the highly skilled craftsmen able to operate an efficient 'on-call' service.

Bibliography

BOOKS FOR FURTHER READING
B. L. Vulliamy, *Public Clocks* (MacMillan, 1828)
E. B. Denison, *A Rudimentary Treatise on Clocks, Watches & Bells.* (reprinted 1850, E. P. Publishing, 1974)
Rev. A. Barry, *Life & Works of Sir C. Barry* (John Murray, 1867)
Sir George Airy, *Autobiography* (1896)
A. Gillgrass, *The Book of Big Ben* (Herbert Joseph, 1946)
F. Ferriday, *Lord Grimthorpe* (John Murray, 1957)
M. H. Port (ed.), *The Houses of Parliament* (Yale University, 1976)
Dr Vaudrey Mercer, *Edward John Dent & his Successors* (Antiquarian Horological Society, 1977)

PAMPHLETS
A. W. Hattersley, *History of the Great Clock & Bells* (Unpublished, 1957)
Alan Phillips, *The Story of Big Ben* (HMSO, 1959)
Various authors, *'Big Ben – Its Engineering Past & Future* (Institution of Mechanical Engineers, 1981)

PAPERS
Parliamentary Papers nos. 257 (1848), 500 (1852), 436 (1855) and 553 (1860)
E. B. Denison, 'Visit to the Westminster Clock' (*Horological Journal*, 1873)
T. R. Robinson, 'Big Ben and Great Tom' (*Horological Journal*, 1957)
T. R. Robinson, 'The Great Westminster Clock Ticks Off a Century' (*Horological Journal*, 1959)
C. K. Aked, 'Westminster' (*Horological Journal*, 1978)

Index